D0520381

Great World Writers

TWENTIETH CENTURY

EDITOR
PATRICK M. O'NEIL

Volume 9

Amos Oz • Alan Paton • Luigi Pirandello

Erich Maria Remarque • Jean Rhys

Mordecai Richler • Rainer Maria Rilke

MARSHALL CAVENDISH

NEW YORK • TORONTO • LONDON • SYDNEY

Marshall Cavendish
99 White Plains Road
Tarrytown, New York 10591-9001

www.marshallcavendish.com

Project Editor: Marian Armstrong
Development Editor: Thomas McCarthy
Editorial Director: Paul Bernabeo
Production Manager: Michael Esposito

Designer: Patrice Sheridan

Photo Research: Anne Burns Images
Carousel Research, Inc.
Laurie Platt Winfrey
Elizabeth Meryman
Van Bucher
Cristian Pena

Indexing: AEIOU
Cynthia Crippen

Library of Congress Cataloging-in-Publication Data

Great world writers : twentieth century / editor, Patrick M. O'Neil.
p. cm.
Vol. 13 is an index volume.
Includes bibliographical references and index.
ISBN 0-7614-7469-2 (v. 1)—ISBN 0-7614-7470-6 (v. 2)—
ISBN 0-7614-7471-4 (v. 3) —ISBN 0-7614-7472-2 (v. 4)—
ISBN 0-7614-7473-0 (v. 5) —ISBN 0-7614-7474-9
(v. 6)—ISBN 0-7614-7475-7 (v. 7)—ISBN 0-7614-7476-5
(v. 8)—ISBN 0-7614-7477-3 (v. 9)—ISBN 0-7614-7478-1
(v. 10)—ISBN 0-7614-7479-X (v. 11)—ISBN 0-7614-7480-3
(v. 12)—ISBN 0-7614-7481-1 (v. 13 —ISBN 0-7614-7468-4 (set)
1. Literature—20th century—Bio-bibliography—Dictionaries.
2. Authors—20th century—Biography—Dictionaries.
3. Literature—20th century—History and criticism. I.
O'Neil, Patrick M.

PN771.G73 2004
809'.04—dc21
[B]   2003040922

Printed in China

09 08 07 06 05 04   6 5 4 3 2 1

Contents

Amos Oz

BORN: May 4, 1939, Jerusalem

IDENTIFICATION: Israeli writer of socially conscious novels that realistically evoke the emotional and spiritual struggles of kibbutz dwellers and urban Jews and explore the conflicting passions of political, scientific, and artistic community leaders.

SIGNIFICANCE: Amos Oz wrote his most popular and critically acclaimed work in the early 1970s. His first novel, *My Michael* (1968), established his importance as an emerging voice in Hebrew fiction. This portrait of a lonely young Jewish woman whose struggling academic husband sacrifices her happiness for his own modest success strongly resonated in Jewish communities. Oz's later novels proved immensely popular in the United States and many other countries worldwide, and his work has been translated into nearly 20 languages. He has received the French Prix Femina and the Frankfurt Peace Prize. His passionate explorations of jealousy, loneliness, and ambition have made him a leading Israeli advocate for peace.

The Writer's Life

On May 4, 1939, Amos Klausner was born in Jerusalem. His father, Yehuda Klausner, was a librarian who always wanted to be a professor of literature. Klausner's family included scholars and educators who emigrated to Israel during the early 1930s from Poland and Russia. Amos remembers that as a child he read a newspaper article written by a leader of the Zionist labor movement who claimed that, once the Jewish state was established, nothing in the world would ever be the same—not even love.

Childhood. The British left Jerusalem when Amos was nine years old. While playing in the dangerous streets of Jerusalem after the war of independence, Amos saw his first corpse: an old Jewish man who was gunned down by sniper fire. This bleakness was balanced by a scholarly atmosphere at home. His parents,

Yehuda and Fania, spoke more than a dozen languages between them. Amos shared the bottom shelf of his father's bookcase from the age of six and became a passionate reader. Sadly, Fania Klausner committed suicide when Amos was 13. During this turbulent time he decided to leave Jerusalem. He boldly made the choice to move from his father's house to Kibbutz Hulda, which would be his home base for the next 25 years. After making the move, he changed his surname to Oz, a Hebrew word meaning "strength" or "courage."

Late Adolescence. The early years Amos Oz spent on the kibbutz were relatively happy. A great deal of his time was devoted to reading American classics by Herman Melville and William Faulkner. He was also interested in the poetry of the seventeenth-century Englishman

A young boy in a cotton field outside a kibbutz carries a bag of cotton that he helped harvest. Picking cotton at Kibbutz Hulda was one of the menial chores that helped the intellectual and literary Oz to become more aware of the simple things in life.

HIGHLIGHTS IN OZ'S LIFE

1939   Amos Klausner is born on May 4 in Jerusalem.

1953   Leaves Jerusalem for the rural life of Kibbutz Hulda; changes his surname to Oz.

1957–1960 Trains with the Israeli army.

1960   Marries Nily Zukerman, a native of Kibbutz Hulda, on April 5.

1961   Completes army service.

1962   First short stories are published in the literary quarterly *Keshet.*

1963   Oz begins studying literature and philosophy at Hebrew University.

1965   *Where the Jackals Howl* is published.

1967   Oz sees active combat in the Sinai; is reserve soldier in tank unit during Six-Day War; is awarded B.A. degree.

1968   First novel, *My Michael,* is published.

1969–1970 Oz becomes visiting fellow at Saint Cross College, Oxford.

1972   Becomes a leading figure in the Israeli Peace Now movement.

1973   Sees active combat in the Golan Heights during the Yom Kippur War.

1975   Is author in residence at the Hebrew University of Jerusalem; *My Michael* is made into a film.

1984   Oz is author in residence at Colorado College.

1986   Wins Bialik Prize.

1990   Is author in residence at the Hebrew University of Jerusalem.

1991   Is elected full member of the Academy of Hebrew Literature.

1992   Is awarded the Frankfurt Peace Prize, as well as France's Prix Femina.

1997   Is admitted to the Légion d'Honneur.

1998   Accepts the Agnon Chair of Hebrew Literature at the Ben-Gurion University of the Negev.

1998   Is awarded the Israel Prize for literature.

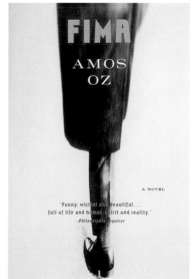

John Donne, as well as the work of S. Y. Agnon, Israel's Nobel laureate. The time that he spent in the cotton fields and working night patrol helped him become even more reflective and develop close ties with nature. Kibbutz Hulda was only three miles from 1967 prearmistice lines, and so the border had to be rigorously patrolled.

The Future Writer. Although Oz was clearly a gifted child, Kibbutz Hulda encouraged individuals to be well rounded, and so he also spent time helping with the more menial chores, including cafeteria duty in the communal kitchen and cotton harvesting. This early contact with the land sustained Oz's intense awareness of the harsh yet poetic potential of the desert well into his early adulthood. Oz first began publishing short stories in the prestigious literary quarterly *Keshet*. The kibbutz recognized his literary aptitude and encouraged him to study humanities at the university.

College Years and Academic Training. After receiving a solid liberal education at the Hulda kibbutz school, Oz went on to study Hebrew literature and philosophy at the Hebrew University of Jerusalem. He graduated in 1967 with a Bachelor of Arts degree and was a visiting fellow at Oxford University during 1969 and 1970, where he read philosophy and English literature.

The Fledgling Writer. Oz began working on his first novel soon after leaving Hebrew University. He wrote *My Michael* from the first-person perspective of a lonely young woman who has almost randomly chosen to fall in love with a young geology student and who lives in a self-destructive catatonic stupor waiting for him to succeed in an academic career. This was an interesting choice of plot and character for Oz's first novel, in light of the death of his mother in his own adolescence and his father's thwarted wish to become a scholar.

The War Years. By the time Oz was in his mid-thirties, he had already produced four successful novels that neither glamorized nor vili-

A group of armed Israeli soldiers, with guns at the ready, march along a road during the Six-Day War. Oz also served in that 1967 Arab-Israeli war as a member of a tank patrol in the Sinai.

fied kibbutz life. He had also served in the Israeli army (from 1957 to 1961) and seen active combat with a tank patrol in the 1967 Arab-Israeli War. His father, Yehuda, died in October 1970. By 1972 he was a passionately dedicated member of the Israeli Peace Now movement.

Success. In 1978 Oz wrote *The Hill of Evil Counsel* and was awarded the Brenner Prize, one of Israel's most coveted literary awards. The community of Hulda decided to give Amos more time to write, although he continued his chores in the field and kitchen. When he became a commercial success in the United States, he donated all his royalties to the kibbutz. Even as he wrote, Oz continued to read American classics, including the work of Sherwood Anderson and the experimental verse of the Beat poet Allen Ginsberg.

Marriage and Domestic Life. On April 5, 1960, Oz married Nily Zukerman, a childhood friend from the kibbutz; their marriage has been very happy and mutually sustaining. Their son, Daniel, and two daughters, Fania and Gallia, all served in the Israeli army. Because Daniel suffered from severe asthma, in 1991 Oz moved with his wife and son to Arad, a desert city in northern Negev in the hope that the desert air would benefit his son. The plan was successful. Oz has remained dedicated to the principles of sharing that were the cornerstone of life on the kibbutz and still donates his profits from his enormously successful novels for the community's well-being.

His Father's Dream. Oz became a professor of literature at Ben-Gurion University of the Negev. He also worked as a writer in residence at the Hebrew University and spent two semesters in 1984 and 1985 as a writer in residence at Colorado College. As of 2003 he was a full professor at Ben-Gurion University of the Negev and still a dedicated member of the Peace Now movement in Israel.

International Advocate for Peace. Oz's work has been translated into over 30 languages. His book of short stories *Where the Jackals Howl* has been in print in many languages throughout the world ever since 1965. *Black Box* (1987) spent more time at the top of Israel's best-seller list than any other novel in history. Oz's novels, which advocate peace, patience, and compromise, have influenced the world. In 1991 he was elected a full member of the Academy of Hebrew Languages. The following year he was awarded the Frankfurt Peace Prize, which was presented by the German president Richard von Weizsäcker. In 1997 President Jacques Chirac of France awarded him the prestigious Cross of the Knight of the Légion d'Honneur. He may yet follow in the footsteps of his mentor S. Y. Agnon, the Israeli Nobel Prize–winning novelist.

Having served on active duty in the Israeli army from 1957 to 1961, and again in the Sinai in 1967 during the Six-Day War, and again in the Golan Heights in 1973 during the Yom Kippur War, Oz turned away from war toward peace. For thirty years he has been dedicated to the Peace Now movement in Israel. Here, members of the Peace Now movement, young and old, hold a torchlight demonstration in front of Prime Minister Ariel Sharon's residence in Jerusalem to protest against war and the occupation of Palestinian territories.

The Writer's Work

Amos Oz has written short stories, essays, novels, and literary criticism. He is, however, known primarily for his novels—particularly those translated into English in the late 1980s and early 1990s. The most conspicuous qualities of these novels are their powerful and provocative descriptions of life in Jerusalem and the Israeli desert. His lean, stark prose provides memorable portraits of the redemptive and destructive potential of restlessness, jealousy, and political ambition.

Issues in Oz's Fiction. Oz once wrote that the "only essays that I do are for rage." Nor is rage, usually restrained, absent from his novels. From his earliest short stories, written in the late 1960s and collected in *Where the* *Jackals Howl,* Oz consistently demonstrates sympathy for domestic and wild animals and a respectful rage for the thwarted lives of women, nomads, and anyone betrayed by false love or duplicitous ambition. He uses various types of animal and human behavior as metaphors—a wild jackal chews its own paw off and swallows the bait in the lockjaw trap, an old woman spends her final days catching stunned flies to feed as special treats to her dead husband's tropical fish—to illustrate "fear, loneliness—all the great and simple things of life and literature."

In May 1949 Israel declared its independence. Oz, only nine years old, had to obey the sunset curfew because the streets were still filled with violence after the war of indepen-

The darkness and anger depicted in Bill Binzen's black-and-white photograph embodies the emotion that most often underlies Oz's writings: rage.

Amos Oz decided after reading a newspaper article written by the Zionist labor movement that he would be happier living in a more rural setting, and so he moved at the age of 14 to the Kibbutz Hulda, which is located between Jerusalem and Tel Aviv, two of the principal cities of Israel.

Oz credits Yosef Haim Brennar as being one of his strongest literary influences. This Hassidic Hebrew writer died in 1921, aged only 40, during combat with Arab forces. Oz notes that Brennar did not achieve lasting fame in Israel or international recognition in the literary world; nevertheless, Oz admires Brennar's use of the Hebrew language and claims that he was one of the first writers to shatter the religious aura and structure of Hebrew. Brennar used the language forcefully and made it work in new ways.

Inspired by Virginia Woolf, the British author of *Mrs. Dalloway* and *To the Lighthouse,* Oz writes standing up at a pedestal desk. He composes first drafts in longhand and, like Woolf, meticulously revises them later on the typewriter. He is not a great fan of the Jewish American writers, except for Saul Bellow, and calls the characters of most other Jewish American writers too wise. John Donne, the English poet, satirist, and elegist, is also a strong literary influence.

The immersion in nature, the emphasis on education, and the sense of community and sharing prevalent in kibbutz life—a life Oz knew from the time he was fourteen—had a strong influence on his writing. Here, a kibbutz class studies in a field in Haifa in 1948.

dence. The night that Israel declared its independence, Oz's father, crying, woke him up in the middle of the night. His father said that, as a schoolboy in Russia and Poland, he had been beaten for being Jewish. He was crying because he was happy that, although the possibility remained that Amos might be beaten at school, it would never be because he was Jewish. Oz

The emotionally confused woman in Frida Kahlo's painting *La Mascara de la Locura (The Mask of Madness)* (Fundación Dolores Olmeda, Mexico City) evokes the women in Oz's works, especially Hannah in *My Michael.*

captures the dangerous tone of this time in his description of the citizens of Jerusalem, people who were forced to live, however reluctantly.

People in Oz's Fiction.

Some of Oz's most memorable characters are those who live reluctant lives even in times of peace. Hannah of *My Michael* is a moving example of a woman who has been emotionally paralyzed and neglects her own development. Eventually it becomes difficult for her even to leave her house. When she does, she is reassured only by her habit of spending dangerously large sums of money on fashionable clothes, which will quickly bore her and be discarded to the chagrin of her economically struggling husband.

Yonathan of *Elsewhere, Perhaps* (1973) has a reasonably contented life on the kibbutz in terms of his material and emotional wants. He is adored by his wife and is absorbed by chess, yet gradually he becomes suffocated. He realizes that such a tranquil life is slowly squeezing life and enthusiasm out of him, and he spends an entire winter working up the courage to run away. Despite the fact that he prides himself on his almost reckless bravery, he waits until he is certain that he has secured Azariah to take his place in his father's beloved tractor shed. Even though he claims that he is filled with rage over the perfect devotion of his wife, Rimona, he spends the whole winter making sure that Azariah will also take his place in the marriage bed. He even waits until he is able to find the perfect small-scale maps to pack in his knapsack before he begins his world voyage, which ultimately takes him no farther than the adjacent desert.

Theo and Noa of *Don't Call It Night* (1994) are ideal examples of characters who enable each other to live extremely reluctant lives. Noa, who has wandered restlessly around the world, becomes physically attracted to the desert-scorched Theo, who prides himself on his detached and brief sexual liaisons with women. Even though civil engineering has long been his primary passion, he swiftly agrees to move out into the desert with Noa, who has vague plans of becoming a high

school teacher. They settle into a suffocating routine and hardly ever sleep in the same bed. Noa is aware of the catatonic trench that they have fallen into and tries to convince Theo to run away with her again. He placates her with food—endless omelets and lovingly prepared salads. Despite the fact that all their goals are withering away, they lack the strength to leave one another and rely on sexual attraction to ease them into old age.

Oz's Literary Legacy.

Oz says that he is determined not to write just about Jewish sorrows. He stresses the importance of writing about the pleasure of love, the meaning of the human condition in general, and the captivating influence of urban and desert landscapes. There is a good-humored patience in his novels and a reassuring hopefulness. No matter how bleak individual landscapes appear to be, over time most conflicts get resolved. Yonathan works out his demons by nearly dying in the desert, Hannah finds comfort in sexual tenderness and simply waits out the boredom of living through Michael's plodding ambition, and Noa and Theo try to piece together their own frustrated lives. In Oz's fiction there is always a home to return to—even the jackal who has managed to get himself trapped is able to consume the bait with enjoyment.

BIBLIOGRAPHY

Balaban, Abraham. *Between God and Beast: An Examination of Amos Oz's Prose.* University Park: Pennsylvania State University Press, 1993.

Goodheart, Eugene. "An Interview with Amos Oz." *Partisan Review* 49, no.3: 351–362.

Grossman, Anita. "An Interview with Amos Oz." *Partisan Review* 53, no.3: 427–438.

Roe, Jacqueline. *States of Fantasy.* Oxford: Clarendon Press, 1996.

Wachtel, Eleanor. "Amos Oz." *Queen's Quarterly* 98, no. 2 (Summer 1991): 424–431.

Wirth-Nesher, Hana. "After the Sound and the Fury: An Interview." *Prooftexts: A Journal of Jewish Literary History* 2, no. 3 (Sept. 1982): 303–312.

——. *City Codes: Reading the Modern Urban Novel.* Cambridge, UK: Cambridge University Press, 1996.

Oz and the Stuff of Fiction

Amos Oz observed, in a 1978 interview with Thomas Lask, that writing is not the same as creating a mirror image of life; it is photosynthesis, not photography. In 1979 he elaborated on this theory and suggested that it is vital to write like a camera that takes in too much light so that the edges of the image are blurred and the film appears to be scorched. In *Under This Blazing Light* he compared the writing of fiction to the photographing of the sun. In 1995, when he extensively revised the essays in *Blazing Light* for a second edition, he did not revise this metaphor.

Oz elaborates upon his view of literature in the wry "A Modest Attempt to Set Forth a Theory," an essay in *Under This Blazing Light*. He begins with a short definition of literature, wherein he suggests that sorrow or suffering is the first required subject. He then offers a new rubric for the proper scope of literature, which he characterizes as a circle of sorrow, starting with the work of Homer and Sophocles and moving up to the seventeenth century with John Donne's ecstatic verses and Shakespeare's insistence on the delicious necessity of love.

Plot is optional in Oz's eyes. Like the modernist Virginia Woolf, who wrote in 1926 that the "inconclusive is legitimate," Oz declares that there may be a plot in good literature, but there just as easily may not be. Though he has an open-ended view of what literature may be, he is deadly certain about what it should not be. Ecclesiastes wrote that there is nothing new under the sun. Oz insists that unless there is a new view of the sun, there is really no point in writing fiction; it would be more useful to write essays or organize political factions.

For Oz the primary obligation of life is to enjoy it. This view resembles Donne's injunction to seize love and sensual pleasure while it is available. Oz suggests that good literature should be a celebration that ranges from the large-scale rage of a thunderstorm to the diffident voice of a child. A standard feature of Greek tragedy is the protagonist's tendency to succumb to a tragic flaw. This flaw, usually quite avoidable, typically appears as hubris—excessive pride. Oz demands that the fiction writer not succumb to the simple trap of pride.

The reader may be reminded of Gideon Shenhav's wish to make a lasting impression on his father and his bucolic community in the whimsical yet tragic "The Way of the Wind." Gideon was unafraid to glide near the power lines and finally threw himself directly upon their white heat rather than continue to feel suffocated in an aerial position above the source of the energy that fueled his small but earnest kibbutz community.

Gideon landed in deadly trouble through a fatal dose of inherited pride. His father was anxious to produce a worthy heir and scorned the flawed product of his merger with a

This photograph, *Sun in Pink Sky,* exemplifies the view of writing fiction that Oz expressed in *Under This Blazing Light*: it is like photographing the sun.

mild-mannered woman. He insisted on getting Gideon permission to join the most dangerous combat unit, the paratroopers. Gideon insisted on providing a lavish spectacle for his father and his mother and all the more humble townsfolk. His insistence on being the last man in the sky accounts for the wind luring him into the live wires. His compassionless father threw stones at his son once it became obvious that Gideon's fear of heights would prevent him from cutting the silk cords. Gideon, unwilling to accept the obvious solution of the dagger or the hollow, optimistic assumption that cutting the cords would not hurl him, wet and anxious, onto the high-voltage wires, rationed his strength and dangled artfully, trusting to his fears.

Oz suggests in "A Modest Attempt" that writing good fiction entails the willingness to dangle directly above live wires. The essay is named after "A Modest Proposal," a famous essay by the British satirist Jonathan Swift, immortalized for the whimsical social commentary *Gulliver's Travels.* Swift was also appreciated for his sharp satirical tongue, evident in "A Modest Proposal," where he slyly suggested that the most expedient solution to the Irish famine was to use the skins of Irish infants to furnish glove factories and their bones to stock the broth pots of the famished nation. Such broad-brush satire captured the attention of otherwise complacent readers. Swift, like Woolf and Oz, argued that obvious anger mars fiction. Oz argues consistently that it is important for the fiction writer to provide a new flavor of suffering, an innovative edge to compromise. It is not enough to simply cut the cord.

Reader's Guide to Major Works

MY MICHAEL

    Genre: Novel
    Subgenre: Domestic tragedy
    Published: 1968
    Time period: 1950s
    Setting: Hebrew University and
        Jerusalem's working-class suburbs

Themes and Issues. *My Michael* established Oz as a writer to be reckoned with and is the work that first earned him worldwide attention. Told in the omniscient voice of Hannah, a depressed poet, it chronicles the lean, dry years of living vicariously through her academic husband, Michael, who is a plodding yet earnest student in geology. His father is as intent as Oz's own was on producing an elite scholar, and as Michael continues slowly to the doctoral level, Hannah sinks deeper and deeper into melancholy. Eventually she becomes afraid to leave the house, unless it is to embark on a wild shopping spree; this behavior alarms the cash-poor Michael, who is living on a teaching assistant's meager salary.

Francis Danby's 1821 painting, *Disappointed Love* (Victoria and Albert Museum, London), of an individual in despair over a disappointment in love evokes the melancholy that overtakes Hannah in Oz's domestic tragedy *My Michael.*

The Plot. *My Michael* is filled with the first-person observations of Hannah, who has fallen in love with Michael simply because he broke her fall on a slippery staircase at the university during her first year there. Despite her landlady's warnings against a hasty courtship, the two become engaged immediately. Just before the ceremony, Hannah accompanies Michael to a kibbutz to visit his relatives and friends, and she is struck by the haunting realization that he is an ordinary man. She realizes that she was charmed by his statement about loving the word *ankle* and by his childlike belief in the abilities of cats to discern good character. She confronts him with his selfishness. In a simple and touching gesture (one that anticipates Theo's enclosing Noa's head under his warm shirt in *Don't Call It Night*) Michael explains that he loves her and wipes the tears from her face.

Shortly after they are married, Hannah drops out of school to care for their faintly antisocial son, who is born soon after the marriage. As time passes, except for one brief, happy interlude at the seashore, Hannah begins to suffocate in her domestic role. Michael retreats into his work and takes on side jobs that are slightly demeaning to compensate for Hannah's spendthrift impulses. Just when Hannah seems on the verge of sinking through the floor of their shabby apartment with despair, Michael finally completes his doctoral dissertation, and they are able to move to a nicer neighborhood with a view of gardens and water. Hannah's devotion and reluctant belief in Michael's scientifically thorough brain are rewarded at the last possible moment, when her soul and creativity can still be salvaged.

Analysis. *My Michael* is a fable of the perils of sacrificing one's gifts for romantic love. Hannah could have been a successful poet and perhaps could also have enjoyed fulfilling romantic love with a more compatible partner. However, she did not listen to the caring advice of others and rushed instead into a relationship that left her with no room but years of regret. Ironically, Michael's relatives accuse Hannah of ruining Michael's career, when the inverse is really the case. The only thing that saves Hannah is patience. Michael, lacking real intellectual insight, has to rely on dogged perseverance to reach his goal. Slowly they claw their way to a decent life. Hannah renounces her reverence for Michael, who, like Yonathan in *A Perfect Peace,* has cheated on her with a vulgar and obvious partner. Their son, a blend of dreams and scientific severity, is an emotional mix of the poetic mother and scientific father, a dangerous hybrid.

SOURCES FOR FURTHER STUDY

Locke, Richard. Review of *My Michael. New York Times Book Review,* May 25, 1972.

Mazor, Yair. *Somber Lust: The Art of Amos Oz.* Albany: State University of New York Press, 2002.

Oz, Amos. "An Autobiographical Note." In *Under This Blazing Light.* Cambridge: Cambridge University Press, 1979, p. 165.

DON'T CALL IT NIGHT

Genre: Novel
Subgenre: Psychological drama
Published: London 1994
Time period: 1970s
Setting: Desert town of Tel Kedar

Themes and Issues. Oz's attention to domestic detail in this sedate thriller is as trenchant as George Eliot's. *Don't Call It Night* sold more than 40,000 copies within the first four months of its publication. Although Oz constantly argues that there is more to life than sorrow and that it is important to focus on love, the shape of romantic love in this novel is concave. Two partners have collapsed within themselves and within each other. The emotional catatonia that Hannah in *My Michael* suffered is spread liberally through many of the characters of this later novel.

The Plot. Noa was once a firebrand. She was very restless in her youth and traveled extensively, only stopping to take on temporary office jobs when she ran out of travel money. During one such stint as an administrative

These still lifes, Henri Delaporte's 1788 oil-on-canvas *Basket of Eggs* (Louvre, Paris) [above] and Edouard Vuillard's 1890 *Still Life with Salad* (Musée d'Orsay, Paris) [below], depict the ingredients of the meals that Theo spends his days preparing for a more-and-more unappreciative Noa in Oz's psychological drama *Don't Call It Night*.

assistant, she meets the handsome Theo, a 60-year-old civil engineer. Although a loner, he sometimes allows himself to indulge in sensual comfort, and women generally find him attractive albeit noncommittal. At the peak of his career, he somehow provokes the ire of his business colleagues, who force him into an early retirement. By this time Noa has seduced him with a combination of sexual charisma and coffee laced with liquor. She convinces him that he should drop the bobtail ends of his career and follow her to the desert, where she vaguely plans on becoming a high school teacher.

Despite the fact that this particular part of the desert, Tel Kedar, reminds Theo of his mediocre career, he agrees to go. Noa is not gracious about this concession and becomes moodier and more demanding the more solicitous and nurturing the ever faithful Theo becomes. Noa stops sleeping in the same room with Theo, who good-naturedly begins to fill his empty evenings with shortwave radio broadcasts. He spends his days tenderly preparing nourishing salads and omelets. Noa becomes more curmudgeonly and resentful of his suffocating attention (in the same way that Yonathan is resentful of Rimona's attention in *A Perfect Peace*). However, she does not make any plans to strike out on her own.

The couple seems destined to fall out of love, conflict gradually whittling away their mutual good will. However, when one of Noa's students commits suicide with a drug overdose, the boy's grieving absentee father arrives at the memorial service and commissions Noa to spearhead a campaign to build a drug treatment center in the conservative desert town. Suspicions gradually arise that he has ties with the underworld. Noa feels very guilty about her detachment from her students and cannot even clearly remember the dead student until his father tells her a story about her having lent the boy a pencil. The father also adds that his son, shortly before his death, wrote his father a letter praising Noa as the only teacher from whom he could learn anything. As Noa's guilt increases, she begins to spend a great deal of time with one of the boy's friends, Tali. This wild child wears toe rings and delights in telling stories of the dead student's romantic interest in Noa, which further compounds her guilt. The prospect of the treatment center enrages the community, and Noa's control of the project falters. Theo intervenes at the last moment and buys the building. Gradually the business tycoon sponsor fades from view. Walks to the abandoned building at night slowly bring the thwarted couple into a comfortable intimacy that will allow their relationship to endure.

Analysis. Oz's fiction allows a default position. There is always a place of comfort that characters may return to, even if they have rebelled and temporarily aroused the anger of loved ones. In a very compelling section near the middle of the novel, Theo places Noa's head under his well-worn work shirt and tells her that he thinks of her as his child. Noa has snubbed his offers to use his old civil engineering contacts to try to secure approval for the doomed drug rehabilitation center, but he never gives up on her. Even though his own career has ultimately amounted to nothing more than a pile of half-conceived blueprints and the well wishes of aging colleagues, Theo is kept youthful by his tireless devotion to Noa. They are like whales who spend the bulk of their time in their own psychological depths, occasionally surfacing at the same time and finding lifesaving comfort in a mutual attraction that never fails them.

This psychological thriller has been a global success and has been translated into a dozen languages, including Romanian and Estonian. Some critics have described the novel as sweet and melancholic, and despite the weighty sequences of domestic angst, there is a warm core of optimism that enlivens the sadness of romantic compromise.

SOURCES FOR FURTHER STUDY

Fuchs, Esther. "The Beast Within: Women in Oz's Early Fiction" *Modern Judaism* 4, no. 3 (Oct. 1984): 311–321.

SHORT FICTION

1965 Where the Jackals Howl
(Artsot ha-tan)

LONG FICTION

1968 My Michael (Mikha'el
sheli)
1971 Unto Death ('Ad mavet)
1973 Touch the Water, Touch
the Wind (La-ga 'at ba-
mayim, la-ga 'at ba-
ruah)
1973 Elsewhere, Perhaps
(Makom aher)
1978 The Hill of Evil Counsel
(Har ha-'etsah ha-ra 'ah)
1982 A Perfect Peace
(Menuhah nekhonah)
1987 The Slopes of Lebanon
(Mi-mordot ha-Levanon)
1987 Black Box (Kufsah she-
horah)

1989 To Know a Woman (La-
da'at ishah)
1991 Fima (Matsav ha-shel-
ishi)
1994 Don't Call It Night (Al
tagidi lailah)
1994 Panther in the Basement
(Panter ba-martef)

CHILDREN'S FICTION

1978 Soumchi (Sumkhi)

ESSAYS AND ESSAY COLLECTIONS

1979 Under the Blazing Light
(Be-or ha-tekhlet ha-
'azah)
1992 "Speech Given for the
Frankfurt Peace Prize"
1994 Israel, Palestine and
Peace

1997 "Beginning a Story"
1999 Essays

AMOS OZ

Panther in the Basement

A NOVEL

"A charming
evocation of a
pivotal moment
in an Israeli
boyhood."
—Newsday

A HARVEST BOOK

Gertz, Nurith. "Amos Oz and Izhak Ben Ner: The Image of Woman in Literary Works, and as Transvalued Film Adaptations." In *Israeli Writers Consider the Outsider,* edited by Leon Yudkin. London: Associated University Presses, 1993.

Lotan, Yael. "A Certain Melancholy." *Modern Hebrew Literature* 9, nos.1–2 (Fall–Winter 1983): 84–86.

Moore, Laurie. "God Is in the Details." *New York Times Book Review,* Sept. 29, 1996.

A PERFECT PEACE

Genre: Novel
Subgenre: Picaresque drama
Published: New York, 1982
Time period: 1965
Setting: Mythical kibbutz near the
Arab border

Themes and Issues. Restlessness pervades *A Perfect Peace.* Almost every character in this novel wrestles with his or her own languid demons. This book was translated into nine languages, including Chinese, in 1999. "A perfect peace" is, aptly enough, a phrase included in both Hebrew and Christian burial ceremonies; it relates to the theme of eventual comfort for even the most tortured souls. Yonathan, the favorite son of the domineering secretary of the kibbutz, Yolek, feels suffocated by his father's attention. His wife, Rimona, is equally attentive. Only his dog, Tia, and chess problems offer him any relief.

The Plot. Yolek urges Yonathan to specialize in repairing the kibbutz tractors. His father's insistence is the breaking point for Yonathan, who resolves to claim his freedom and explore the world. Since Yonathan is an earnest young man, he announces his impending departure to both his demanding father and his hopelessly devoted wife. His father upbraids him for his cowardice and refuses to believe that he will ever have the audacity to leave the secure world of the kibbutz. His wife, taking the news

In Oz's *A Perfect Peace* the restless, unsatisfied protagonist, Yonathan, leaves the security of his kibbutz home and family and sets out on an expedition across the desert. Since he is ill prepared for the trip, he doesn't get far. The subject of Jane Linnell Chance's painting *The Adventurer* (Bonhams, London), who looks more lost and disappointed in the desert than adventurous, mirrors Yonathan's state of mind before he returns to his place in the kibbutz.

in stride, repairs his coat and admonishes him to eat well to prepare for the journey. In the meantime there arrives an eccentric, philosophical young man named Azariah, who is a candidate for an honorable discharge from the army. Naturally gifted at tractor repair, Azariah is slowly and reluctantly befriended by Yonathan, who invites Azariah over to the house to play chess and serenade the couple with his guitar.

Gradually Rimona and Azariah fall in love. Yonathan is completely aware of their feelings for one another and even encourages the match, thinking that Azariah will be a good substitute for Yonathan himself in the couple's marriage bed. Once Yonathan is secure that Azariah will fulfill most of his roles, including feeding his beloved hound, he begins to make serious plans to run away. Rimona has become immersed in African folktales and is now conducting an erotic courtship with Azariah. As Yonathan has become something of a Chicken Little figure, always complaining that the sky is falling, the kibbutz is startled to wake up one day and find that Yonathan has really left.

Despite the fact that he packed well for the expedition, Yonathan neglects to bring the proper amount of water. This elementary miscalculation requires him to head for shelter very soon after leaving the kibbutz at dawn, once the powerful desert sun works him over. He wanders into a desert outpost, where he has a passionate encounter with a female soldier who offers to leave and wander with him. Yet Yonathan wants to remain free and so sets out alone. Undone once again by his water miscalculation, he has to rely on the intervention of an almost lunatic old man, who saves Yonathan from his self-destructive wish to fling himself unprepared into the desert.

Analysis. Patience and compromise are always foremost in Oz's worldview. Even though Yonathan has burned all of his bridges by leaving the kibbutz without permission, he still is able to be forgiven at the end of the novel. After his wild misadventures he returns to his house and is forgiven by all, including Rimona, who is now carrying Azariah's child. Even after the prodigal husband returns, Azariah continues to live in the house. The straight-laced, gossiping community gradually accepts this unlikely threesome. The kibbutz is a remote place where apparently anyone can find a comfortable home.

Even a Russian murderer is accepted by the kibbutz and is given a comfortable shed to live in and hot meals. Like Theo of *Don't Call It Night*, the Russian spends his time listening to the radio, as well as knitting comforters for the people in the community, who gratefully accept the practical gifts since it is cold in the drafty winters and damp autumns. The once tyrannical Yolek, reduced to a speechless invalid, gratefully accepts a blue knitted shawl from the murderer.

Everyone who needs to learns humility in this novel. Azariah learns that he must not delude himself with the egotistical wish to become a prophet and that happiness lies in very practical things. Yonathan faces the fact that the outside world really does not have more to offer than a quiet life with his dog, chess games, and new baby. He also gradually accepts the fact that Azariah gives him much-needed friendship and a bizarre yet necessary brotherly loyalty.

SOURCES FOR FURTHER STUDY

Leonard, John. "What Have We Come Here to Be?" *Nation,* November 11, 1996, pp. 25–30.
Schulman, Grace. "Summer Reading: Fiction That Is Worlds Apart." *New York Times Book Review,* June 2, 1985.

Other Works

"NOMAD AND VIPER" (1965). "Nomad and Viper," the opening story of *Where the Jackals Howl,* can fairly be compared to the British writer E. M. Forster's *A Passage to India* (1924).

This photograph was taken in 1998 in Israel's Negev Desert. The Bedouin with his herd of sheep is reminiscent of the handsome nomadic sheepherder that Geula encounters and later, like a viper, viciously and treacherously endangers in Oz's *Nomad and the Viper.*

In that famous novel, a local Indian doctor, Aziz, is tricked by a visiting tourist, Adela Quested, who accuses him of raping her in the Marabar caves. Only after great suffering and substantial damage to his reputation is he proven innocent. The restless despair of a similar aging and lonely woman, Geula, is the subject of Oz's short story.

Geula has become something of a matronly figure of fun in the kibbutz secretariat, which is struggling to find a solution to the problem of the starving nomads that have invaded their territory. Etkin, the leader of the secretariat, is fond of Geula and has invited her to bring her potent coffee to the meeting. Geula is restless and lonely and takes a walk out into the desert before the meeting. She encounters a handsome nomad and his sheep. They share a cigarette, and she begins flirting with him. Aware of his precarious position as an outsider in the desert community, he declines her advances and vanishes. Disappointed, Geula throws herself on broken glass and begins to plan her revenge.

A vigilante group has been formed after Geula fails to arrive at the meeting. Geula does nothing to stop their plan to raid and destroy the nomads, their livestock, and their children. Oz's sympathy for the disfranchised and homeless is clearly evident in his compassionate portrayal of the nomad, who shares his cigarettes with the spoiled Geula and elegantly offers her a light from a silver lighter. The vulnerable position of livestock is also emphasized, as the

Arturo Ciacelli's *Parachutist,* a work of crayon and pastel on paper, captures the essence of Oz's powerful short story "The Way of the Wind." Like Gideon, the parachutist in the painting, unmoving, hangs suspended above the ochre-red earth, the color of which seems to presage his ultimate doom.

shepherd hurls a goat in anger against a tree after Geula mocks him. The goat is not seriously injured, and Geula intervenes and prevents it from suffering additional harm. Yet ironically, she has become as deadly as the desert viper that coils around her thighs as she waits for the vigilante group to begin their marauding of the vulnerable nomads.

This provocative short story is an excellent example of Oz's commitment to the importance of peace and mediation in Israeli and Palestinian relations.

"THE WAY OF THE WIND" (1965). One of the most powerful short stories in *Where the Jackals Howl,* "The Way of the Wind" has strong elements of Greek tragedy. It is built around the struggles of a domineering father and an anxious, impetuous son. Like Phaeton, who tragically insists on driving the chariot of his father, Apollo, the sun god, Gideon Shenhav is anxious to impress his overly critical and chronically disapproving father, Shimson Sheinbaum.

Sheinbaum, a successful leader of the Hebrew labor movement, deciding late in life that he needs an heir, marries Raya Greenspan when he is 56. Three months after the wedding she gives birth to the much-longed-for son. Paradoxically, Sheinbaum then separates from Raya and insists on living in separate quarters. Gideon, unlike his biblical namesake, proves to be a disastrous disappointment to his father. He spends an unremarkable childhood doing poorly in school, publishing sentimental love poems, and being feeble. It is only in his late teens that he makes a bold move—he joins the paratroopers. Since he is the only son and the only child of the estranged couple, both parents must consent. Raya refuses, but Sheinbaum uses some of his old contacts in the Hebrew labor movement to secure special permission. Finally Sheinbaum can begin to become proud of his heir.

Ironically enough, Sheinbaum's pride in his son's airborne skills leads to his public humiliation. Gideon, anxious to impress his father, decides to release both chutes so that he can be the last one visible in the sky during the local air show. A strong breeze carries him into power lines, where he is suspended for hours to the amusement of some cruel local children. He lacks the courage to cut the parachute cords and is eventually electrocuted. His father watches the whole garish spectacle from the ground and finally throws stones at his son and curses him for his cowardice.

This story is a powerful revision of the Old Testament parable of Isaac and Abraham. Sheinbaum, unlike Abraham, is interested only in public glory and is completely willing to sacrifice Gideon to impress the villagers. Gideon dies a messy, painful, and very public death. Sheinbaum begins to realize his foolishness after the accident and returns to his estranged wife. The elements of Greek tragedy reappear at the end of the story as the bereft Sheinbaum faints in the garden from shock.

Resources

Readers of Amos Oz's work will benefit from a historical overview of Hebrew literature. An excellent sourcebook is *The Great Transition: The Recovery of the Lost Centers of Modern Hebrew Literature,* edited by Glenda Abraham (Totowa, NJ: Rowan and Allanheld, 1985). Another is *Modern Hebrew Literature from the Enlightenment to the Birth of the State of Israel:* *Trends and Values,* by Halkin Simon (New York: Schocken Books, 1970).

Institute for the Translation of Hebrew Literature. This institute hosts a good, encyclopedia-style Web page that provides one of the most comprehensive overviews of Oz's work. Each novel or collection of short stories is listed chronologically within the different countries where editions have appeared. The site also provides links to other Jewish writers and allows the reader to situate Oz historically among his contemporaries. It gives an excellent overview of the truly global scope of Oz's work (www.us-israel.org/jsource/biography/oz.html).

New York State Writers Institute. Oz was a visiting writer at the institute on October 28, 1997. It maintains an excellent Web site that provides an informative overview of his fiction, including statistics on the number of copies each volume has sold, as well as a comprehensive list of the many accolades that Oz has received around the world (www.albany.edu/writers-inst/oz.html).

New York Times on the Web. The *Times* maintains an informative Web site that gives useful summaries and critical overviews of many of Oz's books. It also provides an archive of all Oz reviews and articles that have ever run in the *New York Times Book Review* (www.nytimes.com/books/97/10/26/home/oz.html).

HEATHER LEVY

Alan Paton

BORN: January 11, 1903, Pietermaritzburg, South Africa (now the province of KwaZulu-Natal)
DIED: April 12, 1988, Botha's Hill, Natal
IDENTIFICATION: Liberal South African novelist, short-story writer, and biographer; perhaps the twentieth century's most politically committed novelist writing in English.

SIGNIFICANCE: Until the 1990s political power in the Republic of South Africa, a country with a largely black population, was the monopoly of a white minority. Alan Paton was a fierce opponent of the regime and founded the South African Liberal Party to fight its apartheid system. Far more effective than his explicit political activity was his immensely popular first novel, *Cry, the Beloved Country,* a haunting, religiously devout, and painful account of the cruelty that racial division engendered in South Africa. Although none of his other fiction achieved a similar impact, this one book helped turn world opinion against apartheid, and the regime fell soon after Paton's death.

The Writer's Life

Alan Paton was born in 1903 in Pietermaritzburg, Natal, then a British colony on the east coast of South Africa. Neither parent was highly educated; sadly, his father, James, beat his wife and sons (an experience that turned Paton against corporal punishment for life). Nevertheless, both parents retained a deep Christian faith, a faith based in part on the sublime prose of the King James Version of the Bible, especially the Old Testament, and Paton inherited that faith.

All his later writing was to echo the majestic rhythms of the English Bible, and his passionate and gentle religious convictions shaped what he came to believe and write.

During his childhood Paton, an intelligent and cheerful boy, also discovered the joys of secular literature, delighting especially in Sir Walter Scott, Charles Dickens, and Rupert Brooke.

Paton was educated at Maritzburg College and Natal University College, both white-only institutions. He published poetry, visited England as a representative of South African students, and in 1924 graduated with a degree in physics. He taught at Ixopo High School for White Students and then at a high school in Pietermaritzburg. In Ixopo, Paton fell in love with Dorrie Francis Lusted, whom he married in 1928, soon after she was widowed. The union lasted 40 years and was immensely happy; after her death he wrote an account of their marriage titled *Kontakion for You Departed.*

Reforming Principal. Paton began to achieve national prominence in 1935, when, as the protégé of the liberal politician Jan Hendrik Hofmeyr, he was appointed principal of the Diepkloof Reformatory for young offenders. During the 13 years Paton ran Diepkloof, he introduced progressive reforms, which became controversial as the political tone of South Africa became increasingly reactionary. At the same time Paton became increasingly committed to liberal political causes, including racial equality in his "beloved country."

In the mid-1940s Paton went on a professional tour of prisons and reformatories in Sweden, Norway, and North America. In 1946 in Trondheim, Norway, he began writing his first and best-known novel, *Cry, the Beloved Country,* finishing the book in San Francisco on Christmas Eve the same year. It was published in New York in early 1948 and was an immense critical and popular success throughout

Paton is shown here with his four-year-old son, David, in Pietermaritzburg, Natal, South Africa. At the time, around 1934, Paton was teaching at Maritzburg College. The following year he was appointed principal of Diepkloof Reformatory in Johannesburg.

the world. Almost overnight, Paton found himself famous and wealthy.

Internationally Famous Author. The year 1948 was the turning point of Paton's life. By the time *Cry, the Beloved Country* came out in South Africa in September, the political situation had changed utterly. At the general election in May, South Africa's voters (almost all of whom were white) swept into power the National Party. The Nationalists were committed to total separation of the races in every sphere of life, their goal being the disfranchisement of the blacks and the permanent entrenchment of white supremacy. They were to hold power for four decades, and Paton and his liberal white friends were thrust into perpetual, embittered opposition.

Paton had resigned as principal of Diepkloof as soon as the financial success of his novel was

FILMS BASED ON PATON'S BOOKS

1951 *Cry, the Beloved Country*

1974 *Lost in the Stars*

1995 *Cry, the Beloved Country*

Three years after his appointment as principal of the Diepkloof Reformatory for young offenders in Johannesburg, Paton addresses a group of the young offenders. The boys are candidates for the first free hostels, one of the progressive reforms he introduced in his thirteen-year tenure as principal.

certain. His reforms there were undone almost immediately, and the school was closed within a few years. Now that he was free, he settled with Dorrie at Anerley, an idyllic seaside village in Natal, and their two sons were sent to an Anglican boarding school in Johannesburg. Paton's fame prospered, but his writing did not.

Emotional, short, awkward, vulnerable, intensely pious, Paton was never to achieve another success comparable to the instant success of *Cry, the Beloved Country,* and this comparative failure haunted him. At Anerley he produced a stream of poems and short stories, some of them very good, but no great new novel. He was feted in the United States and England; he was involved with two successful projects inspired by his novel, a film by Alexander Korda (cut by the censors before being shown in South Africa) and a Broadway musical, *Lost in the Stars.* His melancholy increased, however, especially as the apartheid regime continued to impose repressive laws. In 1953 he published a second, much less successful novel, *Too Late the Phalarope.* Then, setting aside full-time writing, Paton founded a colony for blacks with tuberculosis and entered active politics.

The Politician. The South African Liberal Party was formed by Paton and others to oppose the deepening grip of apartheid. Paton was its leading light and its leader from 1956. In practical terms it was a thorough failure, consistently rejected by white voters, who had no desire to share power with the black majority. Nor was its constitutional approach popular with militants on the Left, who experimented with bombings as a mode of opposition. Rather, the party's role was to preserve the conscience of South Africa's

Paton and his first wife, Dorrie, enjoyed a thirty-nine-year-long and loving marriage. Here they are shown with their two sons. The older son, David, is seated, while Jonathan, six years younger than David, is resting his hand on his mother's shoulder.

HIGHLIGHTS IN PATON'S LIFE

1903   Alan Stewart Paton is born on January 11 in Pietermaritzburg, Natal, South Africa.

1914–1918 Is educated at Maritzburg College.

1919   Enters Natal University College.

1920   First poem, "To a Picture," is published in the college's magazine.

1925–1928 Teaches mathematics and chemistry at Ixopo High School.

1927   Friendship with J. H. Hofmeyr begins.

1928   Paton marries Doris ("Dorrie") Francis Lusted at Ixopo (they will have two sons).

1928   Moves back to Pietermaritzburg to teach at Maritzburg College (until 1935).

1935   Is appointed principal of Diepkloof Reformatory, a penal school for black boys, in Johannesburg.

1942   Serves on Anglican Diocesan Commission to inquire into church and race relations.

1943–1944 Writes series of articles on crime, punishment, and penal reform.

1946   Studies penal institutions in Europe, the United States, and Canada; writes *Cry, the Beloved Country* during his travels.

1948   *Cry* is published; National Party comes to power; Paton resigns from Diepkloof Reformatory to live and write at Anerley, on Natal's south coast.

1953   Moves to Botha's Hill in Natal to work in a tuberculosis settlement (to 1955); publishes second novel, *Too Late the Phalarope;* helps found the Liberal Party.

1955   Writes *The Land and People of South Africa* for high school students in the United States and Britain.

1956   Becomes chairman and then national president of the Liberal Party; serves as trustee of the Treason Trial Defence Fund to finance the defense of Nelson Mandela and others facing the death penalty for opposition to apartheid.

1958   Begins a series of articles, "The Long View," in *Contact*, a Liberal Party newspaper.

1960   Opening of his musical *Mkhumbane* in Durban; state of emergency is declared; Paton's passport is confiscated.

1964   *Hofmeyr* is published; *Sponono* has Broadway production.

1967   Paton is widowed.

1968   *Instrument of Thy Peace* is published; Paton is hailed as a significant Christian thinker; the Liberal Party disbands.

1969   Paton becomes founding editor of *Reality: A Journal of Liberal Opinion;* marries Anne Hopkins.

1970   Passport is returned.

1981   Third and final novel, *Ah, but Your Land Is Beautiful,* is published.

1988   Paton dies on April 12 at home at Botha's Hill; second volume of autobiography is published.

Paton with his second wife, Anne Hopkins, on their wedding day in Durban, South Africa, in 1969.

white minority as the regime became more authoritarian. Paton's passport was confiscated in 1960, and his house was raided in 1966. Meanwhile, Dorrie was fading slowly of lung cancer (she died in October 1967). In 1968 the Liberal Party was forced to dissolve under the Prevention of Political Inference Act.

During this period, most of Paton's writing was overtly political, including a strident biography of his old friend and mentor J. M. Hofmeyr.

Later Life. Happiness returned in 1969, when Paton married his secretary, Anne Hopkins, a much younger woman. In 1970 his passport was restored, and his international reputation as a speaker and prophet increased. In South Africa his enemies were now not the government so much as radical blacks, who from 1976 increasingly turned to violence.

In 1980 Paton produced a third and final novel, *Ah, but Your Land Is Beautiful;* two volumes of autobiography followed. He continued to travel around the world, the apartheid regime began to dissolve, and not long after he died at home on April 12, 1988, a majority-rule regime under Nelson Mandela came to power. In an inaugural speech Mandela praised Paton as one of the spiritual founders of the new South Africa.

The Writer's Work

It is impossible to understand Alan Paton without understanding the tragic history of his country in the twentieth century. For the unique catastrophe of South Africa and the unique dilemma that faced South African whites furnished Paton with both raw material and tragic passion. He was a reforming educationalist and reforming politician whose zeal spilled over into literature. His zeal was all the more intense because until after Paton's death white South Africans continued to choose the opposite path, the path of tyranny over the black majority and defiance of world opinion.

South Africa is shared by three distinct peoples. The blacks (mainly Zulus in Natal, Xhosa elsewhere) form a large majority. The Boers, or Afrikaners, are descendants of Dutch settlers who arrived at the beginning of the seventeenth century and still speak Afrikaans, a dialect of Dutch. The smallest of the three groups, the English-speaking descendants of nineteenth-century British settlers, included the Patons.

The year before Alan Paton's birth, the British Empire had triumphed over the Afrikaners in the Boer War, but the first 50 years of Paton's life saw the slow reversal of this victory, with the Afrikaners achieving political power, which they used to break away from the British Empire and to deprive the blacks of all political power and most of their civil rights.

A minority within the English-speaking white minority and a tiny minority of Afrikaners, too, opposed this white supremacist regime but without much success. South Africa's tragedy—the failure of Paton's own people to heal it, the refusal of the Afrikaners to retreat from their monopoly of power, the intensified suffering of the blacks—dominated all Paton's life and was the inspiration of his writing.

Writing was Paton's second career: he had turned 45 before his first significant publication, but his early life had been a long preparation for the novels and short stories. Born to white privilege, he had learned through his

Two film versions of Paton's *Cry, the Beloved Country* were produced forty-four years apart. In the 1995 version actor Richard Harris played the role of James Jarvis while actor James Earl Jones portrayed Reverend Stephen Kumalo.

SOME INSPIRATIONS BEHIND PATON'S WORK

The rough purple mountains, valleyed grasslands, and fragrant coast of Natal where Paton grew up were for him a revelation of the goodness of God. He never lost his awe at the beauty of his beloved country, even where the misgovernment of man spoiled it (as described in the opening chapter of *Cry*). The generous natural beauty of South Africa, he believed, stood as a permanent reproach to human meanness—thus, the beloved country is summoned to cry over human evil—and would in time help cure diseased politics by inspiring a matching generosity in men and women. This theme is particularly strong in *Too Late the Phalarope:* the coming of the phalarope bird (like the coming of the rain at the end of *Cry, the Beloved Country*) is a sign of God's grace and forgiveness, even if people frequently fail to receive it.

The natural beauty of South Africa, like the mountains and grasslands shown here, were an inspiration for Paton throughout his life. The beauty and physical goodness of his "beloved country" gave him hope that these attributes would inspire a generosity of spirit in the people who lived there.

Patterns of racial separation and inequality had been a feature of South African life for centuries before 1948, when an incoming National Party government codified them into the regime of apartheid. Under this system blacks were disfranchised, rigorously divided from whites (as well as from "coloreds," or mixed-race groups, as they are officially designated in South Africa) in every facet of life great and small, restricted from free movement by what were called the pass laws, and legally subordinated to whites in all economic affairs.

Paton passionately opposed the worsening excesses of the apartheid system. He insisted on the opposite ideal of racial togetherness: whites' acceptance of liberty for blacks and blacks' acceptance of the permanent presence of whites. Meanwhile, all his writings are colored by the presence of racial tyranny.

Apartheid so scandalized world opinion that South Africa eventually faced strict economic sanctions (which Paton in fact opposed), and the system was abandoned in 1989. Black majority rule followed.

Born a Methodist, Paton converted to Anglicanism when he married his first wife and was for the rest of his life a loyal and enthusiastic Anglican; he was devout in its practice, he served in its counsels, and he befriended its leaders. His writings reflect his faith, not generically Christian but specifically Anglican, with its rational, mystical, and ethical emphases. It is notable that a good many of his characters—Kumalo, Vincent, and Msimangu in *Cry, the Beloved Country* and Clayton in *Ah, but Your Land Is Beautiful*—are not only Anglicans but Anglican clergymen.

Paton was a liberal, a founder and leader of the Liberal Party, and the spirit of liberalism inspires all his work. Outside the United States being a liberal indicates a commitment to individual liberty over and against the claims of state, church, race, nation, or nationalism; it implies a certain optimism about the ability of individuals to manage their own affairs if left alone by authority. In a specifically South African context, liberalism means freeing people, white as well as black, from the laws that segregated and controlled the races and also from the social conventions that also insisted on separation. Once men were free, Paton believed, they might cease to fear and learn to love each other. This liberal political faith was for him literally inspiring.

The racial tyranny that gripped South Africa under apartheid and the white supremacist regime had a major influence on Paton's work. Shown in these three photographs are the silent symbols of that tyranny—the "whites only" signs that controlled all aspects of life in South Africa: a "whites only" telephone booth, a "whites only" public beach, and a "whites only" taxicab.

years at Diepkloof to love and respect blacks; he had grown up with a deep Christian faith and had perceived a connection between the Gospel and reform of South African society. When he turned to writing, these convictions gave his work a remarkable power and urgency.

How involved ought writers to be in political affairs? How explicitly political ought literature to be? Is a literary work of art better if it has impact on its society? Anglo-Saxon literature is famously more detached from contemporary politics than European writing; Paton is one of the great counterexamples, for the artistic power of his writing is clearly increased by the reader's knowledge that his words are meant to change how people act and did change how many people thought.

Paton's body of fiction consists of three novels, a collection of short stories, and a small body of poetry, some of it light or occasional. Some of the short stories are remarkable experiments in economy, and he is among the more original Anglican poets of the century, but his importance as a writer rests on the novels, especially *Cry, the Beloved Country.* What might have been a mere tale with a message takes on such nobility from its rhythmic plotting, from its borrowed biblical cadences, and from the mysterious beauty of the Zulu language that it must count as one of the most creative novels of the century.

BIBLIOGRAPHY

Alexander, Peter F. *Alan Paton: A Biography.* London: Oxford University Press, 1994.

Callan, Edward. *Alan Paton.* Rev. ed. Boston: Twayne, 1982.

Coetzee, J. M. *White Writing: On the Culture of Letters in South Africa.* New Haven, CT: Yale University Press, 1988.

Daniels, Eddie. "Salute to the Memory." *Reality* 20 (July 1988): 6.

Fuller, Edmund. *Books with the Men behind Them.* New York: Random House, 1962.

Gardner, Colin. "Paton's Literary Achievement." *Reality* 20 (July 1988): 8–11.

Parekh, Pushipa Naidu, and Siga Fatima Jagne, eds. *Postcolonial African Writers.* Westport, CT: Greenwood Press, 1998.

Paton, the Bible, and Literature

The great book of the Paton family when young Alan was growing up, as it had been for millions of English-speaking Protestants for three centuries, was the Authorized Version of the Christian Bible, the King James Version, first published in 1611. It remained important for Paton long after he had become a great and subtle writer. Indeed, no other twentieth-century author so obviously echoes the themes and sound of biblical prose in his writing.

Paton's debt to the Authorized Version is on two levels. His novels resonate with the heft and dignity of biblical language, and all his writing rests upon a vision of humanity that is not just liberal but biblical.

Paton's political convictions and his understanding not only of South Africa but of humanity was profoundly Christian and also profoundly biblical: he saw a certain view of the world emerge from this single sacred text.

Of course, any number of political themes can be read out of or into the Bible. The Afrikaaner nationalists saw a model of their apartheid ideology in the Old Testament's tales of a chosen people conquering a promised land with the aid of the God of Hosts and subduing its heathen inhabitants. Black radicals in South Africa, like slaves in the United States, saw in the Bible's violent legends of exodus and revolt the shape of their own liberation. Paton, though, was consumed by the utopian strain in both Testaments—the mood of aspiration for a new, remade world, where all men are reconciled with God and with each other, a world where the cruelties that make men bitter and eager to commit more cruelties will have passed. The various races and temperaments will accept each other without dread or envy.

The great image in the Old Testament for this remade world is the holy mountain of God, a mountainside of pastoral peace and plenty. The central image for the remade world in the New Testament is the New Jerusalem, the perfect city of peace seen by Saint John in his visions on Patmos and described by him in the Book of Revelation. Paton called the first volume of his autobiography *Towards the Mountain,* and he describes in it how he was consumed by "the vision of John of Patmos, of that world where there shall be no more death, neither sorrow, nor crying," where, in the words of the prophet Isaiah, "the wolf lies down with the lamb and they do no hurt or destroy in all that holy mountain."

This utopian vision would be sentimental and shallow if it did not accept the distance of contemporary mankind from the holy mountain and the painful, patient journey needed to approach it. Certainly, twentieth-century South Africa, with its nightmarish racial divisions and oppressions and its legacy of bloodshed and exile, was almost as far

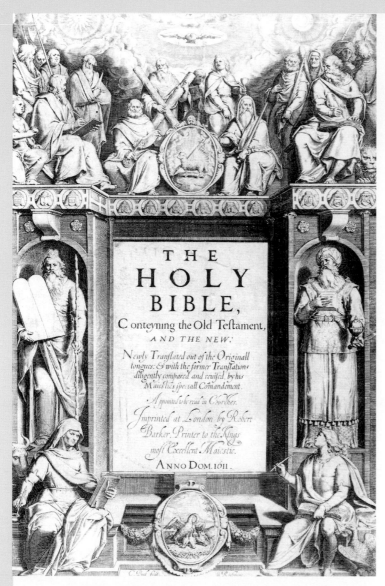

Cornelius Boel's seventeenth-century black-and-white engraving, which appeared as the frontispiece in *The Holy Bible,* published by Robert Barker in 1611, gives an indication of the beauty, dignity, and stately prose of the King James Version of the Bible.

from the New Jerusalem as a society could be. Still, in all his writing Paton urges the possibility of a self-sacrificing pilgrimage out of the hateful morass in which all are born toward a remade world of peace. In *Cry, the Beloved Country* the elder Jarvis is set on the pilgrim's way by the trauma of his son's murder, while old Stephen Kumalo begins to rise out of his dumb resignation.

The English prose of *Cry, the Beloved Country* (and to a lesser extent of the other novels) deliberately echoes the stately language of the 1611 Bible: "Cry, the beloved country, for the unborn child is the inheritor of our fear. Let him not love the earth too deeply"; "There was no water, and everything was dead"; "It was my son that killed your son." Such language is simple, but its repetitions and parallels are more striking than mere urbanity. It can express passions great and raw, ecstasy, and lament, and it sounds timeless, so that *Cry* is, for all its anger, the opposite of a political pamphlet.

The 1611 Bible sounds so serious because it deals with eternal themes in a voice grand enough to seem eternal itself. The reader does not boggle at its claims about the beginning, the shape, and the end of man, because its striking poetic language suggests that it might indeed *know* of such matters.

Paton's fiction looks toward an extraordinary possibility: a harmonious, liberal, multiracial South Africa (one yet to be realized). He announces this vision with the high seriousness of a prophet. He appropriates both an immense biblical perspective and the weighty English associated with the Bible, and he makes these two appropriations one. Paton is not imitating so much as extending the Bible into the modern novel. He suggests to his reader that he not only wants and believes in a new and better future but has actually seen it. The vision is stated in such majestic language that his reader begins to see it, too.

CRY, THE BELOVED COUNTRY

Genre: Novel
Subgenre: Protest fiction
Published: Johannesburg, 1948
Time period: 1946
Setting: Johannesburg, South Africa, and the hill country of Natal

Themes and Issues. South Africa, incomparably beautiful, is sick with fear and hatred on the eve of apartheid: Black tribal society is dissolving; its young men are drifting into the cities and into crime; the whites in panic are contemplating a yet more savage apportionment of power, wealth, and land. Two good middle-aged men, the black Kumalo and the white Jarvis, experience at first hand their country's agony and beauty when Kumalo's son, adrift in Johannesburg, murders Jarvis's son. Absalom Kumalo is hanged, but both fathers have begun to move out of their frozen and doomed positions toward redemption. Their familial suffering is emblematic of national tragedy; their mutual forgiveness and reconciliation suggest hope for the nation's fate. Thus, although the tone of the novel is stylized lament, full of echoes of Zulu speech and of the Authorized Version of the Bible, its final mood is exultation.

The Plot. Book 1, "The Search," begins with a beautiful, lyrical, and consciously biblical vista from the Drakensberg range of Natal, where the soil seems "holy, being even as it came from the Creator"; below, the valley has been ruined, eroded, impoverished and emptied of its young. In the village in the denuded valley, the Zulu Anglican priest of Ndotsheni, the Reverend Stephen Kumalo, rustic, devout, dignified, and venerable, is anxiously receiving a letter from Johannesburg. His brother John, his sister Gertrude, and his delinquent son, Absalom, have all disappeared into that great metropolis that was founded on gold mining. Sure enough, it is bad news: an Anglican priest in Johannesburg, another Zulu, named Theophilus Msimangu, writes to say that Gertrude is sick. Kumalo and his wife tremulously gather up their tiny savings, and he boards a train for the terrible city. His journey is a descent into an urban world that terrifies and overwhelms him. He is cheated, he gets lost, but eventually he reaches Msimangu at the Mission House (which dazes him with its opulence), only to hear that John has become a radical politician and an atheist, while Gertrude has become a prostitute.

Kumalo quickly rescues Gertrude and her boy from squalor, though he is baffled by John's hardness. With the philosophical Msimangu, Kumalo begins a search through the slums and reformatories of Johannesburg. Because of a black boycott of buses, they must walk or be given lifts by friendly whites (who are thus breaking the law). They find Absalom's pregnant mistress, but before they can find him, they learn that black burglars have murdered a wealthy, educated young white, Arthur Jarvis, who was an activist on behalf of South Africa's blacks. As Kumalo fears, Absalom and his cousin, John's son Matthew, are the murderers. "Cry, the beloved country," the narrator says; "these things are not yet at an end." Kumalo, in agony, visits his son in prison and survives a crisis of faith.

In book 2, "Trial and Reconciliation," back in the lovely highlands of Natal at the pleasant farm of James Jarvis, a kindly but politically aloof English-speaking farmer, news arrives of his son's murder. He and his wife fly to Johannesburg, where James begins to grasp his son's Christian idealism about reforming South Africa. The trial begins. In a haunting scene, the shabby Kumalo appears at the door of the house where Jarvis is staying: "It was my son that killed your son." "I understand what I did not understand," replies the ennobled Jarvis. "There is no anger in me." The judge releases Matthew but condemns Absalom, who sobs shamelessly.

A scene from the stage musical *Lost in the Stars,* a musical tragedy inspired by Paton's novel *Cry, the Beloved Country.* The original Maxwell Anderson-Kurt Weill Playwright's Company production ran for about a year on Broadway, from 1949 to 1950. This photograph is from that production.

Kumalo arranges for Absalom to marry his mistress in prison, says farewell to his terrified son, and leaves. Gertrude abandons her own son and returns to prostitution, Stephen and John Kumalo are estranged forever, Msimangu enters a monastery, and Stephen returns to Natal, having failed to save his brother, sister, or son from their various fates but bringing with him a new generation: his pregnant daughter-in-law and his nephew.

In book 3, "Rebuilding," Kumalo is welcomed back to Ndotsheni, where there is drought. His eyes have been opened: he realizes he must act, he must try to save his people. A beautiful and courteous young white boy who wants to learn Zulu gives the starving villagers milk: it is Arthur Jarvis's son, the image of his father. The drought breaks, and the elder Jarvis and Kumalo speak kindly to each other in the decrepit church, taking shelter from the rainstorm. An angry young black agriculturist arrives: the valley will be less poor but more resentful. Jarvis's wife, Margaret, dying, asks him to build a new church in Ndotsheni.

A final chapter, particularly beautifully written, describes the evening and night before the dawn when Absalom is to be hanged. His father climbs a mountain to keep vigil. He meets Jarvis, who says that he was in darkness until he met Kumalo. Good has come of Absalom's crime: love and forgiveness between the races—perhaps too late, though. Is mutual rage and vengeance now inevitable? The old priest wakes in time to weep and greet the fatal sunrise, but when will light come to South Africa?

Analysis. Once Paton had given up schoolmastering, he wrote steadily and profusely for the rest of his long life, and even leading a political party did not stem his production. Yet it was this first major work, his first novel, that enjoyed a success outstanding in the history of twentieth-century publishing. Nothing else he wrote had anything like the political or literary impact, and it will be for this book that he will be remembered as one of the most influential novelists of the age. Paton is lauded as a great writer because of the extraordinary impact of *Cry, the Beloved Country.*

NONFICTION AND ESSAYS

1955 The Land and People of South Africa
1958 Hope for South Africa
1958 The People Wept
1968 The Long View
1968 Instrument of Thy Peace
1975 Knocking on the Door: The Shorter Writings of Alan Paton
1985 Federation or Desolation

NOVELS

1948 Cry, the Beloved Country
1953 Too Late the Phalarope
1981 Ah, but Your Land Is Beautiful

BIOGRAPHY

1964 Hofmeyr
1969 Kontakion for You Departed
1973 Apartheid and the Archbishop: The Life and Times of Geoffrey Clayton, Archbishop of Cape Town

DRAMA

1959 The Last Journey
1960 Mkhumbane, or Village in the Gully (with music by Todd Matshikiza)
1962 Sponono (with Krishna Shah)

SCREENPLAYS

1950 Cry, the Beloved Country

AUTOBIOGRAPHY

1980 Towards the Mountain
1988 Journey Continued

SHORT STORIES

1961 Tales from a Troubled Land

POEMS

1995 Songs of Africa: Collected Poems

This scene is from the 1951 film *Cry, the Beloved Country,* produced by Zoltan Korda and the author, Alan Paton. It shows the marriage of Kumalo's son Absalom to his pregnant mistress performed in jail before he is executed for murder. On the left is Canada Lee, who portrayed Kumalo; on the right is a young Sidney Poitier, who played Theophilus Msimangu.

It is possible for a novel to dramatize a political crisis at just the right moment so that it seizes the public imagination, influences the trajectory of history, and is therefore inevitably hailed as great literature. *Uncle Tom's Cabin,* by Harriet Beecher Stowe, was such a book: a lurid, formulaic melodrama, it appeared so opportunely that it stirred up the North against slavery and was (so Abraham Lincoln said) one of the immediate causes of the Civil War.

Cry, the Beloved Country is extremely effective as liberal (and Christian) propaganda. It moves the reader's mind and heart against the racial injustices of South Africa (and, indeed, of America), compelling him or her to long for reform; it manifests the beauty and courage of the Christian virtues of forgiveness and forbearance. It is not just propaganda, however, and its impact is therefore greater than the impact of *Uncle Tom's Cabin.* There is in this novel a vision of how humans ought to live, a vision that envelops the national crimes and follies of the beloved country. Nelson Mandela, the first black president of South Africa, proclaimed, "*Cry, the Beloved Country* . . . is . . . a monument to the future. One of South Africa's leading humanists, Alan Paton, vividly captured his eloquent faith in the essential goodness of people in his epic work." Paton's thinking is more complex than a belief in man's essential goodness, but Mandela was right about *Cry* being a statement of a complete faith. The *New Republic* declared it "the greatest novel to emerge out of the tragedy of South Africa, and one of the best novels of our time." It is larger than South Africa's predicament.

Kumalo is thus much more striking than Stowe's Uncle Tom: his faith has to grow and not merely endure. He has to surmount his timid, naïve nature not least by grasping that the destruction of the Kumalo family is not just an individual tragedy. It is one small result of the decline of tribal society. White South Africa deliberately wrecks the authority of tribal structures, even of the Zulus, proudest of all tribes, and thus Gertrude drifts into whoredom, John into contemptible rabble-rousing, and Absalom into crime. These personal calamities are not unconnected with the great national struggle, which Kumalo, when he first arrives in Johannesburg and is thwarted by the bus boycott, finds merely baffling. Through suffering and through travel, he becomes stronger and more comprehending, until in book 3 he can seek to redeem the ruined valley.

The character who best understands the tragedy of the beloved country is a man the reader never meets: young, handsome, brave Arthur Jarvis, heroically virtuous and as chivalrous as King Arthur, who illuminates by virtue of his understanding of South Africa and is murdered while writing on the causes of black crime. He has already connected the reforming impulse with personal action, founding and leading a club for African boys. The political and the individual become even more intimately connected in him, for by dying, he shows how intimately politics is linked with the state of his land.

The novel's third hero is James Jarvis, his father, who knew nothing of his son's practical and intellectual daring until after he dies. Reflecting on his son's manuscripts, and meditating on the portraits in his son's study of his two heroes, Jesus and Lincoln, James realizes how blind he himself has been to the cause of justice in South Africa. As far as he can, he follows in his son's footsteps.

The book has an antihero, too, to balance its three heroes: Absalom Kumalo, a weakling and a reprobate, who kills out of bafflement and faces death without courage.

Thus, there is a neat parallel structure of aging fathers and only sons: the fathers at first in repose in Natal, the sons living in Johannesburg amid unguessed virtue (Arthur) and unguessed vice (Absalom); the sons doomed to die before their fathers, the fathers fated to learn of their son's wisdom or crime when it is too late. *Cry* is thus as stately and doom laden as a Greek tragedy—or a biblical tragedy, for that matter: "O Absalom, Absalom, my son, my son," cried King David over his own dead, delinquent boy. Kumalo, too, cries out in despair, "My son, my son, my son."

Yet it is a triumphant story, ending with sunrise on the mountain, with the promise of new generations (Gertrude's son, Absalom's unborn child, Arthur's son) at peace with each other and with their past, and with an amazing unity of love between two representative characters, James and Stephen, whose sons South African history has slain, who have transcended history.

Paton helped turn his great novel into a Broadway musical, *Lost in the Stars,* and into a black-and-white film directed and produced by Zoltan Korda. This carefully paced film, released in 1951, starred Canada Lee as Kumalo, the young Sidney Poitier as Msimangu, and Charles Carson as Jarvis. It remains a splendid piece of cinema, protesting racial injustice not only in Africa but in America and everywhere else but never so insistently as to be shrill or shallow.

Cry was remade as a color film in 1995. Darrell James Roodt directed, the eerie Richard Harris is Jarvis, and the orotund James Earl Jones is Kumalo. Although it was made after the dismantling of apartheid, there is a majestic bitterness about Roodt's version, especially in the searing scenes between the two grieving fathers.

SOURCES FOR FURTHER STUDY

Baker, Sheridan. *Paton's "Cry, the Beloved Country": The Novel, the Critics, the Setting.* New York: Scribners, 1968.

Callan, Edward. *"Cry, the Beloved Country": A Novel of South Africa.* Boston: Twayne, 1991.

Rooney, Charles. "The 'Message' of Alan Paton." *Catholic World* 194 (Nov. 1961): 92–98.

Other Works

KONTAKION FOR YOU DEPARTED

(1969). A *kontakion* is an ancient Byzantine church chant, and Paton had in mind the great Russian "Kontakion for the Departed" when he wrote *Kontakion for You Departed,* a monument to his beloved first wife. That hymn contrasts the dreadful grief of bereavement with the acceptance of suffering and, out of that acceptance, peace and even rejoicing. Paton's strange and striking book does the same, revealing very frankly, in 69 brief numbered passages, the intimacies of a happy marriage and the horror of Dorrie's sickness and death in the fear-ridden South Africa of the 1960s.

TALES FROM A TROUBLED LAND (1961).

Paton's collection of short stories explores the horror and hope of South Africa from the viewpoint of different people and, what is most important in that strange land, different races.

"Debbie Go Home" describes the conflict within a family of coloreds (that is, people of mixed race, white and black; coloreds had a fixed, intermediate legal status under apartheid). A new law has just evicted the father from his profession; will he let his daughter go to a segregated debutantes' ball? The dilemma of coloreds—to accept or resist the regime—is painfully explored, and there is no resolution.

"Life for a Life" is a short story that begins to sound like one of Christ's parables. Enoch, a gentle Christian shepherd, falls victim to an Afrikaner detective, Robbertse, a monster of almost satanic cruelty and race hatred. Enoch is an innocent victim whose murder seems however to hint at the redemption of the land.

"Wasteland," an extremely brief and economic tale, tells in harrowing shorthand, without description, of black gangs. A law-abiding black father (rather like Kumalo in *Cry, the Beloved Country*) is set on by a gang that includes his own son; the father kills his son unknowingly in the dark confusion, and the other brigands callously fling the body away.

TOO LATE THE PHALAROPE (1953).

Paton's second novel, *Too Late the Phalarope,* explores racial arrogance and political inflexibility. Its opening lines recall the rhetorical gloominess of Greek tragedy: "Perhaps I could have saved him, with only a word, two words, out of my mouth. Perhaps I could have saved us all. But I never spoke them." The narrator is Sophie, the protagonist; her nephew, Pieter van Vlaanderen, a white policeman, has an affair with a young black girl, Stephanie—an illegal affair, since all sexual contact between the races had been forbidden by the Nationalists' notorious Immorality Act of 1950. The eventual result is destruction for the Van Vlaanderen family and prison for Pieter, but human redemption is revealed in the person of Nella, Pieter's loyal and anguished wife. The apparent melodrama of the plot is canceled as Paton echoes and imitates biblical language: "But you must not think I judge," proclaims Sophie, "nor must you think I write as a child and ig-

This black-and-white photograph of a mixed-race couple evokes the anguish and despair felt by Stephanie and her white policeman lover, Pieter van Vlaanderen, in segregated South Africa in Paton's *Too Late the Phalarope*.

norant. For I know there is a time to weep and a time to laugh; a time to mourn and a time to dance; a time to cast away stones and a time to gather stones together; a time to embrace and a time to refrain from embracing."

AH, BUT YOUR LAND IS BEAUTIFUL (1981). Paton's third and final novel, *Ah, but Your Land Is Beautiful,* appeared almost three decades after his second. It, too, deals with themes of race, fate, courage, and redemption in South Africa and is set in the late 1950s, the period of Hendrik Verwoerd's government, when resistance to apartheid was being organized by Paton himself and others. This novel is far more experimental in form than *Cry, the Beloved Country* or *Too Late the Phalarope,* being built of parallel life stories, letters, speeches, news reports, legal records, and poems, which abruptly run into each other. It is also daring in mingling fictional characters with real-life historical figures, including Archbishop Clayton and the saturnine Verwoerd himself.

SONGS OF AFRICA (1995). Paton wrote poems all his life; the first was published in 1920, but his collected poetry appeared only six years after his death, when his widow, Anne, assembled and edited all his surviving verse. The quality and tone varies. Some poems are occasional and satirical:

> Sometimes I was a glad lib
> Sometimes I was a sad lib
> No more I'll be a bad lib
> For now I am a rad lib

A "rad lib" is a radicalized liberal. The best poems, however, are the intense religious lyrics in stately free verse, such as "Meditation for a Young Boy Confirmed," written in 1950 for his son Jonathan's formal reception into the Anglican Church:

> You will observe that virgins do not bear
> children, and that dead men are not resur-
> rected;
> . . . you will suffer deep troubling of the
> soul. . . .
> Do not hastily concede this territory. . . .

These writings mark Paton as one of the more interesting Christian poets of the twentieth century.

Resources

The best bibliography for the first half of Alan Paton's writing career remains Lea Bentel's *Alan Paton: A Bibliography* (Johannesburg: University of the Witwatersrand, 1969). Many other resources are available to the interested student.

Academic Internet Sites. There are a number of excellent Paton sites on the Web, with connections to a huge array of lesser pages. The best sites are those of the Swiss EduCeth project, which includes electronic texts and recordings (www.educeth.ch/english/readinglist/patona/), and the Engaged Learning Projects of Illinois (http://collaboratory.nunet.net/goals2000/eddy/Paton/Author.html).

Alan Paton Centre. The global center for study of Paton is this museum, archive, and memorial, which contains Paton's study, virtually in its entirety, and an immense amount of material about his life and times. It is situated on the Pietermaritzburg campus of the University of Natal (http://www.library.unp.ac.za/paton/ahome.htm).

Films. The two movies of *Cry, the Beloved Country* are both good, the 1995 version being the better and more searing (see the discussion above). A fine recent documentary about Paton's writing, *Alan Paton's Beloved Country* (directed by Catherine Meyburgh; Clive Morris Productions), can be ordered from Villon Films (www.villonfilms.com/filmrec.php?queryIndex=4).

Guided Tours. Paton's son Jonathan and Jonathan's son Anthony own a company that offers guided tours of areas of South Africa that are linked with their illustrious forebear. The detailed descriptions of the various tours make fascinating reading for anyone interested in Paton's work (http://www.aptours.co.za).

Scholastic Sites. The best of these sites, with activities and discussion questions about Paton's writing, are those of the San Diego County Office of Education (www.sdcoe.k12.ca.us/score/cry/crysg1.html); Web English Teacher Notes (www.webenglishteacher.com/paton.html); and Simon Says (www.simonsays.com/titles/0684818949/RG_0684818949.html).

Other Sites. Barron's Booknotes on *Cry, the Beloved Country* may be read at the company's site (http://pinkmonkey.com/booknotes/barrons/cryblvd.asp), and famous Paton quotations are reviewed at the Brainy Quote site (www.brainyquote.com/quotes/authors/a/a125173.html). A good account of Paton's place in postcolonial African literature may be found at the University of Florida's Africana Collection site (http://web.uflib.ufl.edu/cm/africana/paton.htm).

RICHARD MAJOR

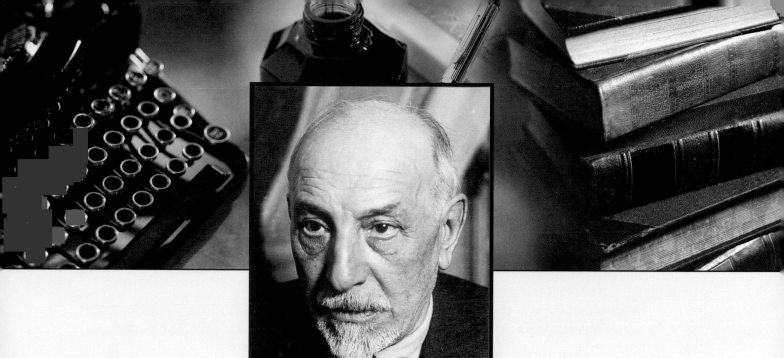

Luigi Pirandello

BORN: June 28, 1867, near Girgenti (now Agrigento), Sicily

DIED: December 10, 1936, Rome, Italy

IDENTIFICATION: Sicilian author of essays, poems, short stories, novels, and plays, in which the received criteria underlying the assumptions of human existence are challenged.

SIGNIFICANCE: Luigi Pirandello shattered the theatrical conventions of post–World War I Europe with his play *Six Characters in Search of an Author* (1921). The play's bizarre situation—a troupe of actors at rehearsal are confronted by six fictional "characters" who claim that they were created by an author who now refuses to complete their story as a proper drama—disrupted the traditional rapport between audience and performer and redefined the boundaries of theater. With this and subsequent works Pirandello became one of the past century's seminal thinkers, a man who forced people to question the very meaning of reality. Pirandello received the Nobel Prize for literature in 1934.

Officially, Luigi Pirandello was born on June 28, 1867, in the city of Girgenti on Sicily's southern coast. However, because his family had sought refuge in the countryside following a serious outbreak of cholera, the writer was actually born in a nearby rural area to which locals had given the name Chaos. In adulthood Pirandello would therefore speak of himself as a "child of Chaos." This statement was both a literal truth and a figurative reference to the fact that his writings sought to reveal the chaos that he believed lay just under the thin veneer of behavior that society usually defines as normal.

Pirandello's father, both volatile and generous in temperament, owned a rich sulfur mine. He wanted his son to become a businessman like himself. Even as a boy, Pirandello resisted. At one point he even went so far as to take the money his father had given him for tuition in mathematics and use it to pay for Latin lessons.

Flight and Reconciliation. In adolescence Pirandello was so unhappy at the prospect of a career in commerce that he actually left Sicily in secret and traveled to Lombardy on the mainland. However, he disliked the idea of having deceived his family and telegraphed his

In 1925 Pirandello directed a production of his play *Henry IV* in Berlin, Germany. Here he poses at the center of the costumed cast during a dress rehearsal.

father to apologize. Happily, his father forgave him and allowed him to stay on in Lombardy to complete another year of high school in his chosen field of study (the humanities).

Palermo, Rome, and Germany. After a time the young student went back to Sicily, completed secondary school, and entered the university in Palermo, Sicily's capital. Pirandello soon decided to leave Palermo, though, and finish his degree in Rome, where the university had more to offer a modern student of literature. In Rome, however, he engaged in disagreements with one of his professors and subsequently chose to finish his degree in Bonn, Germany. Later in life Pirandello was the first to acknowledge that as a student he had been both tenacious and impulsive; these traits account in part for the tortuous path that his studies took.

FILMS BASED ON PIRANDELLO'S WORKS

1932	*As You Desire Me*
1976	*Six Characters in Search of an Author*
1984	*Henry IV*
1984	*Chaos*
1985	*The Two Lives of Mattia Pascal*

Pirandello was born near the town of Girgenti in southern Sicily. In 1927 the name of the town was changed to Agrigento to conform it more closely to the Roman *Agrigentum.* In this photograph Pirandello stands in front of the ruins of the Doric-style Temple of Concord in Agrigento, Italy.

HIGHLIGHTS IN PIRANDELLO'S LIFE

1867	Luigi Pirandello is born in Chaos, on the outskirts of Girgenti, Sicily.
1891	Receives doctoral degree in Romance philology from the University of Bonn.
1892	Returns to Rome.
1894	Weds Maria Antonietta Portulano, also a native of Girgenti, with whom he will have three children.
1903	The Pirandello family's Sicilian sulfur mines fail; Maria Antonietta's mental illness manifests itself for the first time.
1904	*The Late Mattia Pascal* is published to great acclaim.
1919	Maria Antonietta's mental illness requires institutionalization.
1921	Though the premiere in Rome of *Six Characters in Search of an Author* causes an uproar, the play is soon hailed worldwide as a masterpiece.
1922	*Henry IV,* a play on madness, is published.
1923	Pirandello meets publicly with Italy's dictator, Benito Mussolini; establishes his own theater in Rome, the Teatro d'Arte.
1925	Meets and falls in love with a young actress, Marta Abba.
1928–1930	Travels in Europe and America; visits Greta Garbo in Hollywood on the set of *As You Desire Me* (based on Pirandello's play).
1934	Receives Nobel Prize in literature.
1936	Dies in Rome.

In 1891, at the age of 23, Pirandello received his doctorate from the University of Bonn, having specialized in Romance philology (the analysis and authentication of the language or literature of countries where Romance languages are spoken). He immediately began work in Bonn as a lecturer in Italian literature.

Back to Rome. Pirandello soon tired of life in Germany and in 1892 returned to Rome. There he formed a relationship with a fellow Sicilian, Luigi Capuana, an older and established writer who helped Pirandello clarify his own ideas about the purpose and function of literature. Capuana also nudged Pirandello away from the writing of poetry (with which he had previously occupied himself) and urged him to switch to prose. In Rome Pirandello also began married life (he went on to father three children).

Personal and Financial Difficulties. Pirandello had not been back in Rome long when he was confronted by two major crises. First, his family's sulfur mine in Sicily failed and wiped out his financial resources. Second, Pirandello's wife (also a native of Girgenti) began to suffer bouts of mental illness that would torment her for the rest of her life.

To confront the first of these problems, Pirandello turned to teaching to support his family. He also continued his formidable literary production, which grew to include poems, essays, plays, novels, and short stories. The novel *The Late Mattia Pascal* (*Il fu Mattia Pascal*, 1904) marked a significant turning point; it brought Pirandello fame not only in Italy but in other parts of Europe. Eventually, though, it would be his plays rather than his novels that would bring the highest levels of acclaim.

In his private life, however, Pirandello remained virtually helpless in the face of the second crisis, namely, his wife's mental illness. She was unable to cope with the fears associated with her family's change of economic station and soon became the victim of serious delusions. It was not long before Pirandello, though a celebrated intellectual and writer, had to abandon all hope of a "normal" family life.

Changing Times. It is essential to point out, as many critics have, that the changes in Pirandello's private life were mirrored in the tumultuous transformations taking place in the world around him. During his lifetime Pirandello witnessed drastic alterations in politics, technology, and society in general. World War I (in which Italy participated from 1915 to 1918, fighting on the side of its English and French allies) would also affect him deeply; during the war one of Pirandello's sons was held a prisoner for three years.

The Theater. Pirandello's short stories "The Vice" and "The Limes of Sicily" had been refashioned as plays in 1910, shortly before the war. Within a few years Pirandello began writing and producing plays that would define a novel and unique style. The very titles of such works as *Right You Are, If You Think You Are* (*Così è, se vi pare,* 1917) and *The Game of the Parts* (*Il gioco delle parti,* 1918) hint at the provocative qualities of this new phase of his writing.

Scandal and Success. In 1921 Pirandello's masterpiece, *Six Characters in Search of an Author* (*Sei personaggi in cerca d'autore*) was performed for the first time in Rome. Contemporary accounts reveal that audiences expressed wildly different reactions to the play's groundbreaking use of the play-within-a-play structure. Many thought it an artistic scandal, but some months later, when the playwright presented the drama in Milan, it was hailed as a true theatrical success and went on to conquer the stages of the world.

In *Henry IV* (*Enrico IV,* 1922), Pirandello treated the theme of madness, which in real life had so thoroughly debilitated his wife and ruined his chances for a happy family life.

As a result of the international success of Pirandello's work in the 1920s, a group of intellectuals banded together in 1925 to underwrite the founding in Rome of a "theater of art" (Il Teatro d'Arte), which became the home base for repertory productions of Pirandello's old and new theater pieces.

Collections. The sheer number of works written by Pirandello demanded that they be gathered into newly published collections, and among the most noteworthy are the multivolume *Naked Masks* (*Maschere nude,* the collection of his plays that began to take shape in 1918) and the hundreds of tales gathered in the *Novelle per un anno* (literally, "short stories for a single year"), ten volumes of which first began appearing in 1922.

Fascism and Decline. During the last dozen years of his life, Pirandello ostensibly embraced the Italian Fascist government of Benito Mussolini, which had come to power in the 1920s. This unfortunate fact is still a sore point for some readers. Most critics agree, however, that Pirandello's work decidedly defies any sort of interpretation that might be called sympathetic to Fascist ideology.

After the foundation of the Teatro d'Arte, Pirandello's passion for a young actress, Marta Abba, became a source of both inspiration and constant pain for the aging playwright. As divorce was both scandalous and illegal in the Italy of the early twentieth century, Pirandello could never hope to separate from his wife,

Sixty-eight-year-old Pirandello smiles in response to a speaker's comments at a reception held in his honor in Milan, Italy, in 1934, two years before his death.

who still suffered from mental and emotional disturbances.

In his last years of life, Pirandello demonstrated interest in the burgeoning motion picture industry and even went so far as to discuss ideas for a filmed version of *Six Characters in Search of an Author* in which the author himself would be given a role. Pirandello died in 1936 while working on his last play, *The Mountain Giants (I giganti delle montagne).*

The Writer's Work

Pirandello felt that life was essentially a sad and tragic farce, in which people are forced to invent for themselves a sense of reality where none actually exists. One must cling to this sense of reality, even if it is merely an illusion, in order to survive. Without it the constant changes that life throws in one's way would soon overwhelm the mind and the soul.

Pirandello's Worldview.

So long as a man believes in the reality he invents, says Pirandello, he is happy, but once he is made to see through his illusions, his capacity for happiness is seriously diminished. Sadly, the illusory sense of "what is real" is different for each person, and therefore people are at a great disadvantage when they try—either in life or in art—to communicate with one another.

In the Italian tradition Pirandello's pessimistic view (of a world in which those who are happy can remain so only through self-deception) traces itself back to the poet Giacomo Leopardi (1798–1837). Leopardi, too, had insisted that once people discover how cruel fate can be, they can escape the horror of their destiny only through self-deception (that is, illusion).

The critic Olga Ragusa (b. 1922) summed up Pirandello's philosophy as the belief that truth is *always* relative: what one believes to be true depends to a great extent on the individual's situation. Pirandello takes his place alongside other thinkers who, at the end of the nineteenth century and the beginning of the twentieth, pointed to the influence of circumstances on a person's sense of reality. These thinkers included Albert Einstein (1879–1955), who investigated the changing nature of time within the context of natural science, and Sigmund Freud (1856–1939), who insisted that the mind is controlled by unconscious forces that may seriously alter an individual's sense of what is real.

Pirandello the Storyteller.

If Pirandello had simply been a cynic, he probably would not continue to interest readers and theatergoers. His genius lies in his ability to explore the relativity of truth within the structure of familiar

Many of the characters in Pirandello's works exhibit signs of madness or, perhaps, the illusion of madness. His 1922 three-act tragedy *Enrico IV (Henry IV)* raises the question of whether the main character, Henry, has lost his mind or is just trying to make everyone believe he has. In the 1984 Orion Classics film *Henry IV,* based on Pirandello's play, Marcello Mastroianni, shown here, plays the twentieth-century Italian nobleman who awakens from an accident believing himself to be an eleventh-century German king.

forms of realistic narrative. Indeed, his comic, narrative, and dramatic skills are such that his works are, on the surface, quite easily followed. Rest assured, however, that once Pirandello has gotten an audience's attention, he usually goes on to turn some aspect of the story it had expected to hear into a study of brutal realities that are less logical and much harder to define than anyone thought at first.

While Pirandello finds the world harsh and absurd, he still demonstrates great respect for those who must live in it. He himself described the human condition as something to be represented with "bitter compassion." Along with his need to expose the multiple levels of reality on which people exist, Pirandello also displays an overwhelming desire to celebrate the stories of their lives.

Circuits of Communication. As mentioned, one of the hallmarks of Pirandello's philosophy is the emphasis it places on the difficulty of communication. A short play entitled *The Other Son* (*L'altro figlio,* 1923) provides a fine example. In this piece the audience meets a woman, Maragrazia, who is easily identified as insane. All the people in the Sicilian town where she lives treat her as such, apparently with good reason.

Maragrazia rants pathetically and continually about the loss of her two sons, who, like most of the town's young men, have emigrated to the Americas. Illiterate and ignorant, she pays her neighbors to write letters to her faraway sons, never realizing that her neighbors, too, are illiterate; the "letters" they write contain no words, just meaningless lines and symbols.

Maragrazia, the main character in Pirandello's short play *The Other Son,* also appears to be mad. The reason for her illogical actions in denying her "other" son is finally revealed through the efforts of a doctor, a stranger to the Sicilian town where she lives. In this scene from "The Other Son," an episode in the 1984 MGM/UA Classics film *Chaos,* Margarita Lozano, as the mother who does not acknowledge her "other" son, is comforted by the doctor, played by Carlo Cartier.

When a stranger, a doctor, comes to town, he asks the townspeople why Maragrazia, whose pain is obviously real, is shunned by the rest of the townsfolk. "She raves about loneliness, but she has another son right here in town," her neighbors reveal. Indeed, she has a third son, who seeks her love and would be willing to take care of her. Maragrazia is thought to be deranged precisely because she keeps insisting that this other son does not exist.

Finally, the stranger presses her to explain the mystery. In a long flashback monologue Maragrazia recounts how her husband met with a violent death at the hands of some local criminals, one of whom had raped her. The ensuing pregnancy produced the "other son." Maragrazia lives in perpetual torment because this third son—so physically similar to the man who killed her husband and raped her—is a constant reminder of past horrors. She cannot accept the reality of her third son's existence. If she did, she would not be able to bear the pain.

The play is effective not only because it challenges the traditional sense of the seemingly unbreakable mother-son bond but also because it questions the possibility of communication within that relationship. With letters she does not realize are phony, Maragrazia tries desperately to communicate with the two sons she will never see again; meanwhile she turns her back on the third son, still in Sicily, with whom she could speak at any time. In the flashback monologue Maragrazia's voice suddenly becomes a superb instrument of communication and more than compensates for her illiteracy. Her detailed account of her suffering is a powerful narrative that allows the audience to realize that, in her eyes, her third son is not real. Pirandello is able to join his ability as a writer of compassionate and realistic narrative to the talent for inventing dramatic situations that are ultimately strange and illogical.

Pirandello's Art. Any writer with a philosophy as cogent and well thought out as Pirandello's

SOME INSPIRATIONS BEHIND PIRANDELLO'S WORK

All Italian writers of the early twentieth century were influenced to one degree or another by those authors, both French and Italian, who had written in the new realistic and sometimes documentary style that was an important literary development of the late nineteenth century. Among those earlier authors, Luigi Capuana and Giovanni Verga were especially influential on Luigi Pirandello. Both of them, like Pirandello himself, were Sicilian.

Pirandello was also spurred on by another local phenomenon, Sicilian dialect theater, as well as by a more widespread movement called the theater of the grotesque, a "subversive" form of drama that was a forerunner of the theater of the absurd. The theater of the grotesque was markedly antinaturalistic and thus counts as a strong influence on the theatrical works of Pirandello.

Etching of Giacomo Leopardi, an Italian writer who died thirty years before Pirandello was born. Leopardi's writings began an Italian literary tradition that takes a pessimistic view of the world, a world in which only self-deception (illusion) allows people to remain happy. Pirandello reflects this literary tradition in his writings.

Ambroise Tardieu's 1838 engraving *Woman in a Straitjacket* (Bibliothèque de la Faculté de Médecine, Paris) is an illustration in Etienne Esquirol's book on mental illness *Des Maladies Mentales. . . .* The engraving, depicting a woman locked away physically, bodily, and mentally evokes one of the major themes of Pirandello's works: madness.

runs the risk of preaching to his readers or audience. This accusation has been leveled at, among other works, the aforementioned *Right You Are, If You Think You Are.* On stage one meets a group of people who are trying to solve a mystery. Is Mrs. Ponza the person she says she is? Is she an impostor? Is she dead? The audience follows the first two acts as they would any conventional mystery, trying as they watch to guess who is telling the truth. In the third act, instead of an answer Pirandello offers only a deeper mystery. Turning to the audience, Mrs. Ponza explains that there is no solution: she is whoever the audience wants her to be.

Many find this evasive ending highly unsatisfying. Surely, if such an ending was a novelty in 1917, the novelty has by now worn off. However, Pirandello's defenders would claim that audiences can still be made to delight in the ambiguity of *Right You Are*. They would value the subversive nature of the play, which takes its audience to the point of discovery only to mock the theatrical journey by having one of its characters (the victim) declare that the play offers no definitive answer. Here again, Pirandello marries his narrative abilities to a dramatic situation that transports the audience into the realm of what is strange and surreal. This revolutionary approach to theater influenced future writers, such as Samuel Beckett, and the filmmakers Ingmar Bergman and, in a comic milieu, Woody Allen.

BIBLIOGRAPHY

Bassanese, Fiora A. *Understanding Luigi Pirandello.* Columbia: University of South Carolina Press, 1997.

Bentley, Eric. *The Pirandello Commentaries.* Evanston, IL: Northwestern University Press, 1986.

Biasin, Gian-Paolo, and Manuela Gieri, eds. *Luigi Pirandello: Contemporary Perspectives.* Toronto: University of Toronto Press, 1999.

Büdel, Oscar. *Pirandello.* New York: Hillary House, 1966.

Cambon, Glauco. *Pirandello: A Collection of Critical Essays.* Englewood Cliffs, NJ: Prentice-Hall, 1967.

Caputi, Anthony Francis. *Pirandello and the Crisis of Modern Consciousness.* Urbana: University of Illinois Press, 1988.

Di Gaetani, John Louis, ed. *A Companion to Pirandello Studies.* New York: Greenwood Press, 1991.

Giudice, Gaspare. *Pirandello: A Biography.* Translated by Alastair Hamilton. New York: Oxford University Press, 1975.

Nichols, Nina da Vinci. *Pirandello and Film.* Lincoln: University of Nebraska Press, 1995.

Ortolani, Benito, ed. and trans. *Pirandello's Love Letters to Marta Abba.* Princeton, NJ: Princeton University Press, 1994.

Ragusa, Olga. *Luigi Pirandello.* New York: Columbia University Press, 1968.

———. *Luigi Pirandello: An Approach to His Theater.* Edinburgh: Edinburgh University Press, 1980.

ON HUMOR

Genre: Essay
Subgenre: Aesthetic analysis
Published: 1908

Theme and Issues: With his essay *On Humor,* Pirandello defines a theme that will preoccupy him for the rest of his life: the contrast between illusion and reality.

The contrast is demonstrated by a simple example. If a man sees an elderly woman who is trying to look young (by dyeing her hair, wearing inappropriate clothes or too much makeup, and so on), he might laugh because he is immediately aware of the juxtaposition of two opposites (old and young). This observation is comical, but it is not true humor.

Humor comes into play only after the man reflects on why the old woman might be made up in such a fashion. He might decide perhaps that the poor woman is trying to look attractive so that she can hold on to a young husband who dreams of abandoning her. Having considered this possibility, it is difficult to continue laughing at her in the same way. What appeared to be a silly old woman (illusion) turns out to be a sad human being for whom one feels compassion. Reflection has led to feeling, a feeling for the reality behind the illusion.

SOURCES FOR FURTHER STUDY

Illiano, Antonio, and Daniel P. Testa, eds. and trans. Introduction to *On Humor.* Chapel Hill: University of North Carolina Press, 1974.

THE LATE MATTIA PASCAL

Genre: Novel
Subgenre: Narrative fiction
Published: 1904
Time period: Late nineteenth century
Setting: Italy

Themes and Issues. In point of fact, the late Mattia Pascal, the protagonist of the novel of the same name, is not dead. Rather, Mattia (a poor librarian) is the victim of an odd twist of fate. While he is away from home, a corpse turns up in his native town, and the local officials, mistaking the body for that of Mattia, declare him to be dead.

This situation gives Mattia what seems to be a golden opportunity: namely, the chance to change one's identity—to reinvent oneself, as contemporary jargon would have it. Ultimately, however, the novel shows that people are

This photograph, taken in France in 1940 during the Second World War, illustrates the contrast between illusion and reality, the theme Pirandello defined in his 1908 essay *On Humor.* In reality the sentry stands guard by a net camouflage that is hiding a British Royal Air Force plane; yet, the netting gives the illusion of a giant spider web waiting to entice its prey.

doomed to live the lives to which they are born and to exist in the society and culture that fate has determined to be their lot. In short, everyone is a victim of circumstance.

The Plot. Mattia lives in a small town in northwest Italy. Hoping to get away for a while from his unhappy family life (and from a nagging mother-in-law), he takes a trip to the casino at Monte Carlo, where he wins a large amount of money. While returning to his family, he learns from a newspaper that a corpse has turned up in his hometown and that his wife and mother-in-law have identified the body as his own.

Mattia soon realizes that fate has given him the chance to become someone new. He sets off for Rome, where he assumes a new name, Adriano Meis. Soon, though, he discovers that his invented identity is a failure. In terms of official society, he does not exist. He has no pa-

pers, and thus he cannot do anything that requires him to furnish official identification. When he is robbed, he cannot report the crime to the authorities. When he falls in love with a new woman, he cannot marry her.

Having realized that his dream of freedom in a new life can never come true, Adriano decides to fake his death and return home to reclaim his original if uninspiring identity as Mattia Pascal. To his surprise, he finds that his wife has remarried. He is forced to go back to his old job at the library and live out his days as "the late" Mattia Pascal.

Analysis. In taking advantage of the case of mistaken identity that leads his town to believe he is dead, Mattia, rather than escape from his original lackluster self, is in effect trying to steal the one thing no one can ever really have: a new identity. As such, he is in a sense a criminal who

This scene from the 1985 Cinema Italia–Roberto Rossellini production of the film *The Two Lives of Mattia Pascal,* based on Pirandello's narrative fiction *The Late Mattia Pascal,* shows Marcello Mastroianni as Mattia Pascal and Laura Morante as the woman he meets in Rome but cannot marry because he doesn't officially exist.

finally realizes that until he "turns himself in," his life can never truly be his own again.

SOURCES FOR FURTHER STUDY

Stocchi-Perucchio, Donatella. *Pirandello and the Vagaries of Knowledge: A Reading of "Il fu Mattia Pascal."* Saratoga, CA: ANMA Books, 1991.

SIX CHARACTERS IN SEARCH OF AN AUTHOR

Genre: Drama
Subgenre: Absurdist tragicomedy
Published: 1921
Time period: Early 1920s
Setting: A theatrical rehearsal

Themes and Issues: *Six Characters* makes revolutionary use of the dramatic framework known as the play within a play (the same framework used by William Shakespeare in his tragedy *Hamlet* and his comedy *A Midsummer Night's Dream*). In this play the audience encounters two groups, and it must learn to distinguish clearly between the two in order to make sense of the drama.

The first group consists of the actors and the director of a repertory theater company (a company that may produce new plays but often revives plays produced in the past). The director of this troupe is known in the original Italian as the *capocomico,* the chief clown (in English translations the character is usually simply called the director or the producer). Of primary importance is the fact that the director is also something of a jack-of-all-trades. He serves the repertory theater as director, producer, part-time author, and business manager. Along with the director and the actors of the company, the people who work backstage (carpenter, prompter, stage manager) are also part of this first group.

The second group consists of the six characters mentioned in the play's title and also a seventh character, Madama Pace (*pace,* the Italian word for "peace," is pronounced *PAH-chay*), who appears only briefly at one point in the play.

NOVELS

1904   Il fu Mattia Pascal (The Late Mattia Pascal)

1913   I vecchi e i giovani (The Old and the Young)

1915   I quaderni di Serafino Gubbio operatore (The Notebooks of Serafino Gubbio)

1926   Uno, nessuno e centomila (One, No One, One Hundred Thousand)

PLAY COLLECTIONS

1918–1921 Maschere nude (Naked Masks) (4 volumes)

ESSAYS

1908   L'umorismo (On Humor)

PLAYS

1910   La morsa (The Vice)

1910   Lumie di Sicilia (The Limes of Sicily)

1916   Pensaci, Giacomino! (Think It Over, Giacomino!)

1916   Liolà

1917   Così è, se vi pare (Right You Are, If You Think You Are)

1918   Il berretto a sonagli (Cap and Bells)

1918   Il gioco delle parti (The Rules of the Game)

1921   Sei personaggi in cerca d'autore (Six Characters in Search of an Author)

1922   Enrico IV (Henry IV)

1923   L'altro figlio (The Other Son)

1925   La giara (The Jar)

1930   Questa sera si recita a soggetto (Tonight We Improvise)

1930   Come tu mi vuoi (As You Desire Me)

1979   I giganti delle montagne (The Mountain Giants)

SHORT STORY COLLECTIONS

1922–1937 Novelle per un anno (10 volumes)

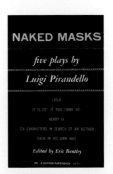

NAKED MASKS

five plays by

Luigi Pirandello

LIOLÀ
IT IS SO! IF YOU THINK SO
HENRY IV
SIX CHARACTERS IN SEARCH OF AN AUTHOR
EACH IN HIS OWN WAY

Edited by Eric Bentley

In 1988 Robert Brustein radically adapted Pirandello's dramatic masterpiece *Six Characters in Search of an Author,* changing the setting from a small Italian town at the beginning of the twentieth century into a contemporary urban-American setting. This photograph shows five of the six characters: in the background, the Stepdaughter (Pamela Gien) and the Father (Alvin Epstein); in the foreground, the Little Brother (Matthew Dundas), the Mother (Priscilla Smith), and the Little Girl (Dawn Kelly).

Shortly after the actors of group 1 assemble for a rehearsal, they are interrupted by the six characters of group 2, who wander in and proceed to disrupt all sense of normalcy. The characters claim to have been invented by an author (obviously Pirandello) who has refused to write their play, that is, has refused to tell their tale on the stage. Two of the charac-ters, the father and the stepdaughter, are most anxious for the director of the company to mount a production that will tell their story. Thus begins a sort of game between the actors and the characters, a contest in which each group tries to convince the other that it has the clearer understanding of what is invented and what is real.

Inside Pirandello's ingenious framework, the audience is permitted to observe not only the characters but also the actors, who function onstage as a second audience. In this way Pirandello's play creates three levels of reality, interposing the reality of the actors (on stage) between that of the characters (also on the stage) and that of the audience (in the auditorium).

The Plot. The characters have a rather conventional story to tell, something along the lines of a soap opera or romantic novel. They convince the company's director to take on the role of author; the director agrees to write their story down as a play to be performed by the actors. At first the director is quite intrigued by the possibility. The characters begin to recount their story in flashback, even going so far as to demonstrate to the actors how the lines should be spoken and how the story should be acted out. Pirandello mines these encounters between characters and actors for all the humor they can provide.

The characters' tale unfolds. The father and the mother had a son. Shortly thereafter, however, the mother fell in love with an office assistant who worked for her husband. The father reacted to this situation with gentle understanding (or so he would have everyone believe) by letting his wife go off to another city to make a new life with his assistant. Together the wife and the assistant have three more children, known in the play as the stepdaughter, the little boy, and the little girl. The father remains alone.

A number of years pass. The father has become middle-aged ("too old to be attractive to women but too young to put them out of his mind"). One day he seeks sexual comfort with a prostitute. Though he does not realize it, the prostitute he encounters is his stepdaughter. The stepdaughter has turned to prostitution because she, her mother, and the other children were left impoverished after the death of the assistant. The father and the stepdaughter come very close to engaging in a quasi-incestuous act.

They are stopped only by the arrival of the mother, who of course is horrified by the discovery that her daughter and her husband are about to have sexual intercourse. The father now feels great shame; to compensate for his moral failing, he takes the family back to live with him again.

The son is so angry that he refuses to talk with anyone in the family. The stepdaughter wants only to run away from the whole situation. In the end the two youngest children are neglected; as a result, the little girl falls into a garden pool and drowns, and the little boy takes a gun and shoots himself.

As noted above, the audience witnesses not only this retelling of the characters' story but also the conflicts that arise as the director and the actors try to rehearse the characters' story. The characters are not at all satisfied with the ways in which the actors try to play out the story. Ultimately, the director and the father cannot come to an agreement on how the story should be told. Indeed, the father at times makes it clear that he wants to be the author. The characters are in torment. On the one hand, they want their story told; only a thorough airing of their story will release them from their odd state of artistic limbo. On the other hand, the characters cannot quite accept the fact that any dramatization of their story (especially by actors as inept as the ones they have encountered) would reduce and release the pent-up fury that they cling to, precisely because it defines their identities so clearly.

Analysis. The great achievement of *Six Characters* is that it manages to maintain the fiction that the six characters are somehow both less real and more real than the fictional creations one usually encounters in a novel or a drama.

How is it that at times the characters seem less real? As Pirandello himself explained, they cannot exist—even as fictional characters—without a drama that tells their story: without a drama, the characters will pass out of existence. (Of course, they do have a drama—the play *Six Characters* itself. The novelty of this play is that it leaves the audience feeling as if the characters have no play of their own.)

How do the characters manage at other times to seem more real than normal dramatic figures? Freed from the constraints of a play that unfolds in a conventional way (from beginning to middle to end), the characters (especially the father and stepdaughter) are free at any point in the show to return to the past, free to bring up the events from their story that still haunt them, free to relive pain that still needs healing. In this sense they are very much like real people who are tormented by the battle between intellect and passion, the very battle that Pirandello himself claimed was also the source of his own torment.

SOURCES FOR FURTHER STUDY

Firth, Felicity, trans. "The Author's Preface to *Six Characters in Search of an Author*." In *Pirandello: Collected Plays*, vol. 2. New York: Riverrun Press, 1988.

Other Works

"CIAULA DISCOVERS THE MOON" (1924). A short story set in a Sicilian sulfur mine, the kind the Pirandello family once owned, "Ciaula Discovers the Moon" describes the harsh lives of miners whose work subjects them to the danger of bodily injury, primarily from the ever-present possibility of explosions.

At nightfall an older miner (who has already lost his son and the sight in one eye to an explosion) decides that, because he intends to stay the night in the sulfur mine, he must let his family in town know that he is safe. He orders his dim-witted assistant, Ciaula, to return to town and carry the message.

When he is in the mines, Ciaula has no fear of the dark; he does not tremble at the strange shadows that the lanterns cast in the caves where the sulfur is mined. He is, however, afraid of the "dark of night," that is, of the dark that he must pass through between the mine and the town.

As he climbs out of the mine, Ciaula is filled with terror. Suddenly, a silver light appears. At first, he believes he is seeing the very last light

William Turner's watercolor *Loch Duich, Summer Moonlight* exemplifies Ciaula's thoughts and feelings on seeing the moonlight when he emerges from the mine terrified and finds peace and beauty.

of dusk. Soon, though, the light becomes so strong that he wonders if perhaps the sun has reversed course and decided to rise again.

All of a sudden, Ciaula realizes that the light is being cast by the moon, "grand and tranquil, as if floating in a cool and luminous ocean of silence." Never before has this simple soul given much thought to the moon. Now it lights his way, banishes his fear, lightens his burden, and causes him to weep tears at its beauty. Sometimes—just when one expects nature to be at its cruelest—it comes up with a surprise.

Yet, Pirandello notes, the moon is completely unaware of the valleys and plains that it illuminates on the earth below. In this way the story invites comparison with the poetry of the aforementioned Giacomo Leopardi, who also depicted the moon as a sort of companion to human suffering, even as he came to acknowledge the moon's (and hence, nature's) indifference to human affliction.

THE JAR (1925). In *The Jar* a Sicilian landowner purchases an enormous earthenware jar, wide enough for a man to stand in and large enough to handle the great quantity of olive oil that the landowner expects his olive trees to produce. Soon after the jar is delivered, workers notice that it is cracked. The landowner is fit to be tied and becomes obsessed with the idea that the jar must be fixed.

He calls in a local repairman who is reputed to have a special glue that will repair the huge jar and make it like new. The landowner argues that the glue alone is not good enough and demands that the repairman also "stitch" the crack with a sort of wire to ensure that it holds together. The repairman finally agrees, but to stitch the jar properly, he has to drop himself down into it so that he can make the repair from the inside. As fate would have it, the repairman gets stuck in the jar.

A comical stalemate ensues. The repairman

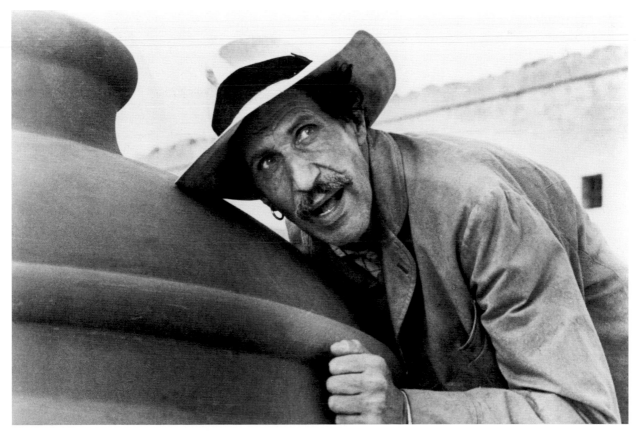

Another episode in the 1984 MGM/UA Classics film *Chaos* was based on Pirandello's play *The Jar.* In this scene from the film, Don Lollo, the wealthy owner of an olive grove (played by Ciccio Ingrassia), hugs the enormous terra-cotta jar he has purchased to hold the tremendous amount of olive oil he expects his grove to produce.

wants to break the jar so that he can get out alive. The landowner, however, insists that the jar must not be broken. After a standoff involving a true battle of wits, the landowner becomes so frustrated that in anger he kicks the jar as hard as he can. It rolls down a bank, crashes into a tree, and breaks, and frees the repairman. The repairman's patience has indeed paid off.

This tale, with its emphasis on the importance of persistence, recalls stories from the oldest Italian tradition, such as the novelle, or short stories, of Giovanni Boccaccio (1313–1375). One of the most famous of these medieval stories involves a huge jar in which a wife hides her lover from her unwitting husband.

Both "Ciaula Discovers the Moon" (which recalls the moon poetry of Leopardi) and *The Jar* (which brings to mind the stories of Boccaccio) demonstrate that Pirandello was keenly aware of the Italian literary tradition. His intention, even in a major work such as *Six Characters,* was not to overturn the tradition but rather to add to it a new dimension, an emphasis on the continual antagonisms of man against man and man against nature, which run in cycles of enmity and apparent reconciliation.

Resources

The Pirandello Society, with headquarters in Middle Village, New York, is dedicated to keeping Luigi Pirandello's memory alive and to fostering critical study of his work. The society's official journal is entitled *PSA*, and it also has a fine Web site (http://pirandello.homestead.com/).

Nobel E-Museum. This site includes texts of the Nobel committee's presentation speech, as well as Pirandello's acceptance speech, as these were delivered when the writer was awarded the Nobel Prize for literature in 1934 (www.nobel.se/literature/laureates/1934/).

Pirandello Home Museum and Library. This institution, near Agrigento, welcomes visitors interested in the writer's origins. Information about the museum and about Pirandello's life in Sicily can be found in English at the museum's Web site (www.regione.sicilia.it/bbccaa/Dirbenicult/engpirandello.htm). The site also gives information about the Pirandello Library, where thousands of manuscript pages (scripts, letters, drafts, and the like) are made available for study by qualified scholars.

Random Web Searches. If the name of a Pirandello play (*Six Characters,* for example) is typed in the "find" box of any of the major Internet search engines, dozens of "hits" will come up, many presenting program notes or reviews of specific productions. This type of search reveals, among other things, how frequently Pirandello's plays are produced around the world. It is wise to remember, however, that producers regularly take liberties with the text of Pirandello's plays, often changing settings, characters, and even plot. While it may be fascinating to see how Pirandello's works have been updated, one should recall that Pirandello's stage directions and lighting and costuming demands were extremely precise. Thus, the text of a particular production described on a Web site may differ greatly from Pirandello's text as originally published.

DAVID CASTRONUOVO

Erich Maria Remarque

BORN: June 22, 1898, Osnabrück, Germany
DIED: September 25, 1970, Locarno, Switzerland
IDENTIFICATION: Popular German writer best known for *All Quiet on the Western Front,* one of the most famous antiwar novels ever written.

SIGNIFICANCE: Erich Maria Remarque's greatest literary success came in 1929 with *All Quiet on the Western Front,* which graphically depicts the horrors and brutality of the First World War through the tragic experiences of a group of young German soldiers. As a fitting tribute to the generation that perished in the war, the book became an immediate international best-seller. Remarque's subsequent novels never attained the same lasting fame, yet they addressed some crucial issues in German history, including the experiences of anti-Nazi émigrés and the Holocaust. The author's lasting significance may derive less from the literary merits of individual novels than from their efforts to grapple with some of his century's tragic events.

Erich Paul Remark was born on June 22, 1898, in the German city of Osnabrück, the second child of Peter Franz and Anna Maria Remark. His older brother, Theodor Arthur Remark, died at the age of five in 1901. His sisters, Erna and Elfriede, were born in 1900 and 1903, respectively. Three years prior to the author's birth, Peter Franz Remark, a bookbinder by trade, had moved from his hometown of Aachen to Osnabrück with his young wife. More than a century earlier, his ancestors had migrated from France to Aachen, where their name was changed from Remarque to Remark.

Youth and World War I. As a child Remarque developed a keen interest in nature, collecting both butterflies and fish, and displayed a deep fascination with the visual, written, and musical arts. His ability at the piano and organ was to provide him with a source of some income during and after the First World War. After attending parochial schools, Remarque enrolled in a Catholic training school for teachers in 1915, where he would remain until he was conscripted into the German army. It was during this time that Remarque made his first foray into fiction as a member of a literary

Erich Maria Remarque (right), not much more than 30 and famous enough to draw a Hollywood studio chief all the way to Berlin. Splendidly dressed and smoldering for the camera, Remarque has sold the rights to *All Quiet on the Western Front*; the buyer is Carl Laemmle (left), president of Universal Pictures. Remarque would sign many more such deals, but he'd never equal the book he had written. A career beginning with ad copy and feeble prose poems had led to an antiwar novel that skeptics dismissed as literary flash. The book's cold detail and understated compassion proved them wrong. The ex-soldier said writing *All Quiet*—in six frantic weeks—brought him "release." Readers made the book into a phenomenon and then a classic.

clique around Fritz Hörstemeier, a local artist and writer.

World War I played a crucial role in Remarque's development as a writer and a person. In November 1916 Remarque, along with a number of his classmates, was conscripted into the German army. After a period of military training, his unit was sent to the western front, where Remarque took part in the fighting in Flanders. In July 1917 he was wounded by shell fragments during an artillery attack. After a lengthy convalescence he returned to active military service in fall 1918. Fortunately for him the signing of the armistice several weeks later signaled the end of hostilities in Europe. Remarque's experiences, including the loss of some of his comrades, made a strong impression on the young man and would later serve as inspiration for *All Quiet on the Western Front*.

Early Career. Remarque returned to Osnabrück, where he completed his training as a teacher. His career in teaching was, however, short lived, and he began working at a series of

FILMS BASED ON REMARQUE'S WORKS

1930 *All Quiet on the Western Front*

1937 *The Road Back*

1938 *Three Comrades*

1941 *So Ends Our Night*

1947 *The Other Love*

1948 *Arch of Triumph*

1955 *Der letzte Akt*

1957 *A Time to Love and a Time to Die*

1977 *Bobby Deerfield*

1979 *All Quiet on the Western Front*

1985 *Arch of Triumph*

Mired in the mud at Flanders. Remarque never got sent to the front line, but comrades looked on him as a good soldier who kept his head. He learned about gun smoke's taste, turnip stew and horse flesh, the "long, nude tails" of rats grown fat on bodies, and rigging a metal lid and a candle to kill lice. His experience made *All Quiet on the Western Front* hypnotically believable.

HIGHLIGHTS IN REMARQUE'S LIFE

1898 Erich Paul Remark is born on June 22 in Osnabrück, Germany.

1916 His first story, *Von der Freuden und Mühen der Jugendwehr* (Of the joys and efforts of the youth defense brigade), is published; Remarque is conscripted into the German army to serve in World War I.

1917 Serves on the western front; in late July is wounded by shrapnel and hospitalized until fall 1918.

1919 Completes educational training as a Catholic schoolteacher; obtains first teaching position.

1920 First novel, *Die Traumbude* (The dream booth), is published; Remarque resigns teaching assignment; works as an organist in the chapel of a state mental institution and as a tombstone salesman.

1921 Becomes theater critic for the local press in Osnabrück; begins using the name Erich Maria Remarque.

1922 Moves to Hannover, where he serves as an editor and writer for the *Echo-Continental*.

1925 Moves to Berlin, where he writes for *Sport im Bild*; marries the German actress Jutta Zambona.

1927 Begins writing *All Quiet on the Western Front,* which he completes in some five weeks.

1929 *All Quiet on the Western Front* is published in Germany, sells more than a million copies, and is quickly translated into almost 30 languages; Remarque divorces Jutta Zambona.

1930 Film adaptation of *All Quiet on the Western Front* has U.S. premiere in May and months later is banned in Germany.

1931 *The Road Back* is published; Remarque purchases a villa in Switzerland.

1933 Leaves Germany on January 29, the day before Hitler becomes chancellor; goes into exile in Switzerland; on May 10 the Nazis publicly burn his works.

1937 Film adaptation of *The Road Back* has U.S. premiere; Remarque begins romance with the film actress Marlene Dietrich.

1938 Remarries Jutta Zambona to prevent her from being returned to Germany; the Nazi regime revokes Remarque's German citizenship; *Drei Kameraden (Three Comrades)* is published.

1939 Remarque departs in August for the United States; joins the German exile community in Los Angeles and New York.

1941 *Liebe deinen Nächsten* is published (it appears in English as *Flotsam*); Remarque begins relationships with the actresses Greta Garbo and Lupe Velez.

1943 On December 16 Remarque's younger sister, Elfriede Scholz, is beheaded in Berlin, following her conviction by the Nazi People's Court for making anti-Nazi and "defeatist" remarks.

1944 Remarque works on report for the OSS detailing methods of reeducating the German population after the war.

1945 *Arc de Triomphe (Arch of Triumph)* is published.

1947 Remarque becomes a U.S. citizen.

1948 Returns to Switzerland.

1952 *Der Funke Leben (Spark of Life)* is published in the United States and Germany.

1956 *Die letzte Station (Full Circle)* is staged in Berlin; *Der schwarze Obelisk (The Black Obelisk),* is published.

1957 Remarque divorces Jutta Zambona for the second time.

1958 Marries the American film star Paulette Goddard; the film version of *Zeit zu leben und Zeit zu sterben (A Time to Love and a Time to Die),* in which the author appears as an actor, premieres.

1961 *Der Himmel kennt keine Günstlinge (Heaven Has No Favorites)* is published.

1962 *Die Nacht von Lissabon (The Night in Lisbon)* is published.

1967 West German government awards its highest medal of honor to Remarque.

1970 On September 25 Remarque dies of heart failure in Locarno, Switzerland.

1971 *Schatten im Paradise (Shadows in Paradise)* is published posthumously.

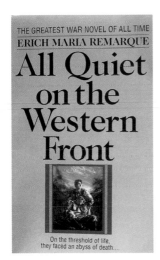

THE GREATEST WAR NOVEL OF ALL TIME

ERICH MARIA REMARQUE

All Quiet on the Western Front

On the threshold of life, they faced an abyss of death....

---

odd jobs, including as an organist and a tombstone salesman. The early postwar period witnessed the publication of his first novel, *Die Traumbude* (The dream booth), and a series of poems and other fictional writings. In 1922 he relocated to Hannover, where he took a position as a writer and editor for *Echo-Continental,* a magazine owned by the Continental Rubber Company. Three years later he moved to Berlin, where he wrote for the popular sports magazine *Sport im Bild.* From 1922 on, Remarque earned his living from the fruits of his pen.

Privately Remarque lived the life of a bon vivant, enjoying the German capital's raucous nightlife, as well as fast cars, nice clothes, French impressionist artwork, Oriental carpets, Chinese bronzes, and the company of beautiful actresses, including his first wife, Jutta Zambona.

Literary Success. In 1929 Remarque scored his greatest and most lasting success with the novel *Im Westen nichts Neues (All Quiet on the Western Front)*. It quickly became an international best-seller, earning him accolades from the liberal and leftist press for the work's pacifist stance and hatred from conservative nationalists and Nazis, who viewed it as an assault on Germany's honor. Awash in this literary and commercial success, in 1931 Remarque published a second novel touching on the experiences of German soldiers in the Great War, *Der Weg zurück (The Road Back)*. The work highlights the disillusioning experiences of ex-servicemen who find it difficult to readjust to peacetime civilian life in the Weimar Republic, Germany's postwar democracy.

Exile. In 1933 Remarque was forced by the rising tide of Nazism to flee his native Germany for the relative calm and security of Switzerland, where several years earlier he had purchased a lakeshore villa once owned by the nineteenth-century painter Arnold Böcklin. He left Berlin just one day before Adolf Hitler was appointed chancellor on January 30, 1933. Viewed as persona non grata by Germany's new rulers, Remarque was publicly denounced, and his works consigned to the flames during the fiery book-burning spectacles staged throughout the country in May 1933. Some five years later he was stripped of his German citizenship. He spent his remaining days outside Germany, except for occasional trips made after the Nazis' defeat in 1945.

Weil, portrayed by actor Larry Blake, pleads with soldiers not to fire on a group of hunger marchers; in the confusion he will end up the only man dead. After writing about the Great War, Remarque turned in *The Road Back* to the turmoil in Germany after defeat. Director James Whale and Universal Pictures made the country's near revolution into a movie when they adapted Remarque's novel in 1937. Weil, a Jew and pacifist, loses his life to soldiers led by one of his old comrades from the war. Their commander shrugs off the mistake. "That does not enter into it," he says. "Only the purpose—law and order."

Exile dramatically affected Remarque's literary output, shaping his themes and hardening his anti-Nazi message. Unlike other refugee German writers, such as Bertolt Brecht, Leon Feuchtwanger, and Heinrich Mann, whose politics were ardently leftist, Remarque remained a bit of a lone wolf, a liberal-minded pacifist who had little sympathy for the Soviet Union or communism.

Though he lost much of his German-speaking audience when the Nazis banned his books, his novels, in translation, continued to find readers in the United States and elsewhere. Unlike many of his fellow exiles, Remarque did not suffer a significant loss of fame or fortune when he left Germany. Major publishers still printed his work, magazines (notably *Collier's*) serialized his new fiction, and Hollywood continued to film his novels.

World War II. As war clouds overshadowed Europe in 1939, Remarque once again made a fortuitous decision to flee, just days before the outbreak of World War II. In the United States he divided his time between Los Angeles and New York; he romanced film stars, including Marlene Dietrich, Greta Garbo, and Lupe Velez, and enjoyed the two cities' vibrant nightlife. In 1944 he penned a report for the Office of Strategic Services (OSS), the U.S. foreign intelligence organization, in which he advocated a strong policy of postwar reeducation of the German population, which he felt needed to be exposed to the crimes of the Nazis and the evils of militarism.

In 1948 Remarque returned to Switzerland as an American citizen. His works were once again published in Germany, although they frequently received negative criticism and were revised to edit out politically unpalatable passages. In 1958 he married an American film star, Paulette Goddard, with whom he remained until his death in 1970.

On the night of May 10, 1933, the new regime rids Germany of some 20,000 books considered dangerous to the Aryan cause. Remarque's novels were among them. The Nazis had singled out the writer three years before, a campaign that hit a climax of sorts when they threw stink bombs and set loose mice to break up a showing of *All Quiet on the Western Front*'s movie version. The Nazis said Remarque slandered the warrior spirit by showing soldiers who just wanted to survive, not be heroes; Remarque said the Nazis were looking for publicity from his book sales. Later he remarked to writer Thomas Mann, "It's more by luck than good judgment that I am on the side I now stand on. But I know that it happens to be the right one." He left the country before Hitler took power, and he would never be a German citizen again.

The Writer's Work

Although Erich Maria Remarque was primarily known as a novelist, his literary output included short fiction, plays, and even a screenplay. Still, it was the writer's novels, particularly *All Quiet on the Western Front,* that earned him international acclaim. Throughout all his work Remarque employs a grandly realistic treatment of both his characters and his settings to illustrate the horrors of war and political repression while reaffirming the author's sympathy for the average man.

Issues in Remarque's Fiction. Remarque uses his characters to personify and explore the evils that societies can impose on their citizenry. It is for this reason that *All Quiet on the Western Front* is regarded not merely as a character study or a work of genre fiction but as one of the foremost antiwar novels of the twentieth century.

Remarque's other novels fall into several different thematic categories. *The Road Back, Three Comrades,* and *The Black Obelisk* treat the issue of soldiers returning home from the First World War and the difficulties they face in readjusting to civilian society. The second series of works, *Flotsam, Arch of Triumph,* and *The Night in Lisbon,* all deal with German refugees fleeing Hitler. A third category of works discusses conditions inside Nazi Germany during the Second World War and is best exemplified by *Spark of Life* and *A Time to Love and a Time to Die,* as well as by his screenplay *Der letzte Akt* (The last act), which recounts the final days of Adolf Hitler and is based upon the book *Ten Days to Die,* written by the noted judge Michael Musmanno, who served on the American military tribunal that tried the leaders of the *Einsatzgruppen,* the special killing units associated with the elite security force, the SS.

In some of his post-1933 fiction, such as *Flotsam, Arch of Triumph, The Night in Lisbon,* and *Shadows in Paradise,* Remarque dramatized the pain and suffering of the anti-Nazi émigrés, their often ambivalent feelings toward Germany, and their sometimes difficult adjustments to life in exile. In two other novels, *Spark of Life* and *A Time to Love and A Time to Die,* he was among the first and most prominent German writers to address Nazi mass murder, the concentration camp system, and the issue of the population's culpability in these crimes. Certainly his own experiences and those of his friends shaped his portrayals of the exile community, while his discovery in 1946 of his sister Elfriede's execution by the Nazi People's Court in December 1943 deeply affected his work.

Characters in Remarque's Work. Remarque's fiction is marked by strong character development; in fact, the realistic nature of his characters is quite remarkable. The author's work resonated with many readers in the aftermath of World War I, because the way his characters meld realism and sentiment reflected both the horrors of the war and the close comradery that developed among the soldiers that fought in the conflict.

In his exploration of man's inhumanity to man, instead of focusing on a specific individual's capacity for savagery, Remarque uses his characters to examine the impact of the politically powerful on average people. This impulse is best exemplified by *All Quiet on the Western Front,* wherein the horrors of war are portrayed and its atrocities and carnage are vividly recounted. *Spark of Life* similarly examines the Holocaust and the concentration camps through the eyes of the imprisoned.

Literary Legacy. At the core of Remarque's legacy is *All Quiet on the Western Front.* The novel will endure as one of the great explorations of the folly of human conflict and the toll that war takes on individuals and society. Remarque's other works complement his masterpiece by expanding on the pain and alien-

Remarque carries Marlene Dietrich's coat. The writer and the movie star knew each other in Berlin and fled Europe together just before World War II. Remarque said they remained friends and no more, but others were not convinced. "Never fall in love with an actress," Remarque supposedly complained to the playwright Clifford Odets. Looking back, Dietrich would write that Remarque's melancholy and sensitivity bordered on the pathological: "I was deeply moved by this trait of his personality. Our special relationship all too often, unfortunately, gave me an opportunity to witness his despair." While the star of *The Blue Angel* sold war bonds and entertained GIs, Remarque wrote *Arch of Triumph* and dedicated it "To M. D."

After decades as a best-selling author and celebrity, Remarque wound up on camera in the adaptation of his *A Time to Love and a Time to Die*. He played Pohlmann, who in the novel voiced his creator's hopes for a civilized future: "Humanity has not advanced in an even course. It has always been only by thrusts, jerks, relapses, and spasms. We were too arrogant; we thought we had already conquered our bloody past." Slouched against the wall is Douglas Sirk, the director of the 1958 film.

ation inflicted by totalitarian regimes on individuals and families. Remarque's books would inspire a generation of writers and serve as the basis for nearly a dozen films, including the brilliant 1930 version of *All Quiet on the Western Front*. Though his fiction documents human brutality, it also depicts the strength and compassion of his characters. It is a rare author who can reconcile these opposing aspects of mankind in powerful and moving prose.

BIBLIOGRAPHY

Baker, Christine R., and R. W. Last. *Erich Maria Remarque*. Oxford: Berg Publishers, 1979.

Cernyak-Spatz, Susan E. *German Holocaust Literature*. New York: Peter Lang, 1989.

Eksteins, Modris. "War, Memory, and Politics: The Fate of the Film *All Quiet on the Western Front*." *Central European History* 13, no. 1 (Mar. 1980): 60–82.

Gilbert, Julie. *Opposite Attraction: The Lives of Erich Maria Remarque and Paulette Goddard*. New York: Pantheon, 1995.

Gooch, Herbert E., III. "Isolationism in *All Quiet on the Western Front*." In *Realpolitik: Political Ideologies in '30s and '40s Films*, by Beverly Merrill Kelley, with John J. Pitney Jr., Craig R. Smith, and Herbert E. Gooch III. Westport, CT: Praeger, 1998, pp. 95–113.

Harris, Frederick J. *Encounters with Darkness: French and German Writers on World War II*. New York: Oxford University Press, 1983.

Kamla, Thomas A. "The German Exile Novel during the Third Reich: The Problem of Art and Politics." *German Studies Review* 3, no. 3 (Oct. 1980): 395–413.

Schwarz, Wilhelm Johannes. *War and Mind of Germany*. Frankfurt: Peter Lang, 1975.

Taylor, Harley U., Jr. *Erich Maria Remarque: A Literary and Film Biography*. New York: Peter Lang, 1989.

Reader's Guide to Major Works

ALL QUIET ON THE WESTERN FRONT

Genre: Novel

Subgenre: Antiwar novel

Published: Berlin, 1928
(in serial form); 1929

Time period: 1916–1918

Setting: Western front in World War I

Themes and Issues. *All Quiet on the Western Front* is Remarque's best known and most popular novel. Composed in a matter of weeks in 1927, the work is a brilliant depiction of the horrors and tragedy of war. The author's goal was not to paint the First World War as an adventure but to pay tribute to a "generation of

A photograph from 1917. Soldiers learned to live in trenches that looked like graves. Remarque described how a man under fire could sink himself in mud and feel grateful to it: "his only friend, his brother, his mother . . . we, thy redeemed ones, bury ourselves in thee." All that counted was to stay alive.

men who, even though they may have escaped shells, were destroyed by the war." As such, it reflects the author's personal experiences at the front and his ardent pacifism in the 1920s. Told through the voice of its main character, Paul Bäumer, the story recounts the individual and collective tragedies of a group of young German soldiers. Like many of his later works, this novel emphasizes the bonding that takes place between people brought together by war and politics. The novel's title, *All Quiet on the Western Front,* carries more than a touch of irony, since this German military phrase, used in reports to indicate no major activity, is issued on the day that the work's main character, Paul Bäumer, is killed.

The Plot. Set during the First World War, the novel details the experiences of a group of young German soldiers on the western front. The main character and narrator, Paul Bäumer, had enlisted in the military along with his classmates Müller, Leer, and Albert Kropp at the age of 18. Serving together in the Fourth Infantry, the youths soon share the bonds of friendship and comradery with Tjaden, a locksmith; Haier Westhus, a peat digger; Detering, a peasant; and a grizzled 40-year-old veteran, Stanislaus Katczinsky (Kat), who mentors the boys, educating them in the ways of survival and scrounging up food from the devastated countryside. The lads soon discover that the visions of wartime glory and heroism that their schoolmaster, Kantorek, had drummed into their heads are pure illusions. The first artillery bombardment and the death and dying that accompany it cure them of these fallacies.

The brutality of war quickly ages Paul Bäumer and his comrades, forever destroying their youthful dreams. The direct confrontation with death, through hand-to-hand combat with the enemy and trench warfare, makes returning to the happiness of the recent past impossible. The youths encounter their wounded comrade Kemmerich in the hospital; he is suffering from the ravages of a fatal wound that has robbed him of his leg. Hardened by life at the front and realizing that his friend will soon die, Müller covets Kemmerich's fine English boots, which cannot help the dead but may ensure the survival of the living. The now mature soldiers educate the new incoming recruits, who experience bouts of fear and claustrophobia as they face the prospect of mass death.

Granted 17 days of leave, Paul Bäumer returns home to see his dying mother, but he feels out of place, as if in a foreign world. The townspeople still talk of final victory and annexations, while Paul has no such illusions of German success, knowing that the enemy, with fresh reinforcements and weaponry from the United States, possesses the military advantage. He realizes that he has changed, not the town. The war has made it impossible for him to recapture his youth.

Returning to the front, Paul confronts death head-on when he mortally wounds a French soldier. As the soldier slowly dies, Paul listens to the gurgling in the soldier's throat and watches the expression of fear on his face. Paul begs for the Frenchman's forgiveness, realizing that the enemy is no different from Paul himself or his comrades. He discovers the identity of the dead man and sees photographs of the soldier's wife and children. Paul pledges to fight against war, which has struck both of them down.

One by one Paul's comrades become casualties of war. Detering flees, only to be court-martialed; Müller dies from a stomach wound; Kropp is sent to the hospital to have his leg amputated; and Kat is killed as Paul carries him from the battlefield. By fall 1918 Paul is the only survivor among the seven recruits from his class. In October, just prior to the armistice ending the hostilities, Paul is killed. That day the German military report contained one sentence: all quiet on the western front.

Analysis. The publication of *All Quiet on the Western Front* was a dramatic turning point in Remarque's literary career. Almost immediately he became internationally known, and his novel was quickly transformed into a Hollywood movie. His savage depiction of war resonated with readers throughout the world, challenging

In *All Quiet on the Western Front*, Paul describes sitting on the battlefield with Katczinsky, cooking their dinner in the middle of the night: "We are two men, two minute sparks of life; outside is the night and the circle of death. . . . I see behind him woods and stars, and a clear voice utters words that bring me peace . . ." The painting is Christopher R. W. Nevinson's *A Star Shell,* exhibited in 1916.

the viewpoints of those nationalist authors who glorified the life in the trenches and blamed Germany's loss on socialists, Jews, and liberals, who allegedly stabbed the country in the back and robbed it of final victory.

Remarque's novel pointed to the futility and brutality of war, the fundamental humanness of all the combatants, and the complicity of those schoolteachers and propagandists who eagerly sent a generation of youths to their death. Using his own experiences as a guide, the author graphically depicted the violence and horror of the First World War through the eyes of young soldiers. Not surprisingly, the novel generated intense controversy in Germany at a time when the Nazi Party was making strong electoral gains. Rather than demonize the enemy and trumpet the values of imperialist aggression, Remarque stressed the commonality of suffering and death. The French soldier Duval serves as a fitting counterpart to the Germans, a simple man forced by his country's government to fight in a war he neither created nor desired. In contrast, the figure of Kantorek symbolizes the pedant who talks of glory and coerces his pupils into enlisting, while remaining safe at home. Like the military, the schoolmaster represents the voice of authority that demands unconditional loyalty.

As he was to do in many of his subsequent novels, Remarque pointed to bonds that held a group together, whether frontline military experience, challenges of life in exile, or prisoner solidarity in a Nazi concentration camp. Paul Bäumer and his comrades know little of life, except despair, death, and fear, and along with the rest of their generation share the same experience, the business of killing and the challenge of survival.

All Quiet on the Western Front remains the author's best-known and best-appreciated work. It serves as a staple in high school curriculums throughout the United States, and the vibrancy of its message and language continue to resonate.

SOURCES FOR FURTHER STUDY

De Leeuw, Howard M. "Remarque's Use of Simile in *Im Westen nichts Neues*." *Erich Maria Remarque Jahrbuch/Yearbook* 4 (1994).

Eksteins, Modris. "War, Memory, and Politics: The Fate of the Film *All Quiet on the Western Front*." *Central European History* 13, no. 1 (Mar. 1980): 60–82.

Schwarz, Wilhelm Johannes. *War and Mind of Germany*. Frankfurt: Peter Lang, 1975.

Taylor, Harley U., Jr. *Erich Maria Remarque: A Literary and Film Biography*. New York: Peter Lang, 1989

SPARK OF LIFE
   Genre: Novel
   Subgenre: Political fiction
   Published: New York, 1952
   Time period: Spring 1945
   Setting: Mellern concentration camp

Themes and Issues. Dedicated to his sister Elfriede, who was put to death by the Nazis for making "defeatist" remarks, *Spark of Life* is a dramatic depiction of life and death in a German concentration camp on the eve of the prisoners' liberation. Remarque began work on this novel in January 1946, less than a year after the Allied defeat of Nazi Germany and less than two months after the International Military Tribunal began proceedings against the major Nazi war criminals in Nuremberg. The liberation of Nazi concentration camps and the gruesome revelations about hideous atrocities and medical experiments carried out at these sites profoundly affected the author. As he began working on the novel, he also first learned about the fate of his sister.

Spark of Life is one of the first postwar German novels to examine the Nazi concentration camp system. As such, it sought to remind Germans of the crimes that the Nazis perpetrated against political prisoners, Jews, and others. The story is set in the fictional camp of Mellern, a site no doubt modeled on the Buchenwald concentration camp, which was liberated on April 11, 1945, by prisoners and American troops.

The Plot. The novel begins in March 1945 with 509, a longtime political prisoner in the Nazi concentration camp of Mellern, trying to

SOME INSPIRATIONS BEHIND REMARQUE'S WORK

Like most writers, Erich Maria Remarque drew upon his own experiences for inspiration, though none of his characters is completely autobiographical. His military service in World War I dramatically shaped his political perspective and the literary flavor of *All Quiet on the Western Front* and *The Road Back,* two novels that focus on male comradery in the trenches amid death and dying and on how the brutalities of war alter human lives. Some scenes in these works appear to come directly from his own experiences at the front or in the hospital. Likewise, his exile from Germany influenced his novels after 1933. Remarque modeled several of his characters upon real-life figures, such as Betty Stern, whose literary salon in Berlin he had attended as a budding author, and various lovers in his life.

From his youth an avid reader of both German and world literature, he was fascinated by the works of Goethe, Proust, Dostoyevsky, Nietzsche, and even the American Jack London. Remarque's strong interests in automobile racing and art, particularly French impressionist paintings and Chinese bronzes, also are reflected in his work.

Remarque in May 1961 with Paulette Goddard, his wife and a star of 1940s Hollywood. Remarque may no longer be the driver of race cars, but he still loves Europe's choicer spots—for example, Piazza San Marco in Venice. He would say he never enjoyed writing until old age: "Ever since the doctor has tried to prevent me from writing, the whole business has acquired something dangerous and attractive."

survive until liberation. After years of incarceration, he had suppressed all hope of freedom, but now, with the Allied air raids on the nearby town and the din of not-too-distant fighting, he realizes that liberty is at hand. Hope returns along with the consuming fear of death. The struggle for daily survival has even deadened his hatred of the town, whose church spires and factories the prisoners could see from the camp. A scrap of bread was more important than anything else.

The political prisoners, realizing that the end of the war is quickly approaching, begin to organize armed resistance to the SS guards, whom they fear will murder them before liberation. Under the brutal and harsh conditions in the concentration camp, solidarity had played a key role in saving some inmates from certain death, such as 509 and another inmate who has gone mad believing that he is a sheepdog. The "popular front" existing between the camp's various political factions, however, shows signs of unraveling. The humorless

communist prisoner, Werner, urges 509 to join the "party" because the coalition of camp factions will be ended at liberation, but 509 opposes the substitution of another totalitarian order over German society and refuses to join, fearing that the communists will apply the same methods of torture, killing, and camps to squelch opposition.

The camp's SS officials, too, realize that the war will soon be over and plot their survival. The camp commandant, Neubauer, who has enriched himself by extorting the wealth of businesses owned by the town's Jews, calculates his financial losses from the bombings and contemplates buying up property for his postwar life in a new Germany. His wife and daughter have already fled with their portion of the ill-gotten loot, yet he decides to surrender the camp to the Americans in true military style, believing that he will be treated correctly and soon released. To disguise the true nature of the camp and enhance his own chances for survival, Neubauer wants gardens planted,

NOVELS

1920 Die Traumbude (The dream booth)
1929 All Quiet on the Western Front (Im Westen nichts Neues)
1931 The Road Back (Der Weg zurück)
1938 Three Comrades (Drei Kameraden)
1941 Flotsam (Liebe deinen Nächsten) (literally, "love thy neighbor")
1945 Arch of Triumph (Arc de Triomphe)
1952 Spark of Life (Der Funke Leben)
1954 A Time to Love and a Time to Die (Zeit zu leben und Zeit zu sterben) (literally, "a time to live and a time to die")

1956 The Black Obelisk (Der schwarze Obelisk)
1961 Heaven Has No Favorites (Der Himmel kennt keine Günstlinge)
1962 The Night in Lisbon (Die Nacht von Lissabon)
1971 Shadows in Paradise (Schatten im Paradies)

SHORT STORIES AND ESSAYS

1916 Von der Freuden und Mühen der Jugendwehr (Of the joys and efforts of the youth defense brigade)
1918 Ich und Du (You and I)
1924 Über das Mixen kostbarer Schnäpse (On the mixing of expensive drinks)

SCREENPLAYS

1954 Der letzte Akt (The last act)

PLAYS

1964 Full Circle (Die letzte Station) (literally, "the last station")

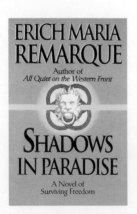

ERICH MARIA REMARQUE
Author of
All Quiet on the Western Front

SHADOWS IN PARADISE
A Novel of Surviving Freedom

new clothing distributed, and better food rations allotted to the prisoners. Other SS officers discuss procuring false papers and joining the communists or rehearse their defense of only acting under orders. Still others hope to get rid of the prisoners before liberation.

As the American troops approach the camp, the prisoners launch the uprising, during which 509 is killed. Liberation brings immediate joy, but it is tempered by a sense of loss, loneliness, and despair many feel as they depart the camp. The oldest prisoner, named Ahasver (after the "wandering Jew" of legend), gives 509 a proper burial. Bucher, a young prisoner who has fallen in love with Ruth, an inmate from the women's camp, leaves Mellern carrying 509's message "to bear witness and to fight." The couple finds a bombed out home, where they can build a new life in a Europe shattered by war.

Analysis. *Spark of Life* represented a bit of a departure for Remarque, as it was not directly or indirectly based upon his own personal experiences. Whereas his novels about exiles concerned people whose plight he shared, knew, and understood, portraying life and death in a Nazi concentration camp was rather different. In creating the novel, he drew upon accounts by former camp prisoners and the vast store of information that was uncovered when the Allied armies liberated Germany. The graphic accounts of American encounters with the Nazi concentration camps in April 1945 made a powerful impression on Remarque, as did the belated news of his sister's 1943 execution the following year.

As in *All Quiet on the Western Front* and his exile novels, *Spark of Life* dramatically depicts the lives of individuals from a variety of backgrounds who are thrown together by external circumstances and share the common bonds of suffering and survival. In this particular case the prisoners' resistance against the SS guards culminates in a camp uprising. In common with some of Remarque's other work, this novel stresses the destruction of the characters' prior world and the inability to return to the status quo ante. Several prisoners, including 509, Ahasver, and the "sheep dog," have irrevocably lost their former identities, and their life in the camp has boiled down to pure survival.

Spark of Life represents one of the earliest attempts by a German writer to confront the issue of Nazi war crimes and the Holocaust. Although the novel does not take place in an extermination camp, it makes a number of references to the Nazi's murder of Europe's Jews, and the brutality of the SS is well depicted. Nor did Remarque neglect to make some comments about the German knowledge of Nazi atrocities. By situating the camp close to a town, whose buildings were close enough to be seen by the prisoners, the author was forcing German readers to confront the crimes that occurred in their midst. The reactions of the local community to the camp prisoners working outside the camp range from turning their heads away to hiding the truth to murder. Remarque also pointed to the economic benefits for local Nazis, some of whom despoiled Jewish citizens of their property to enrich their personal coffers, a type best represented by the camp commandant, Neubauer.

SOURCES FOR FURTHER STUDY

Cernyak-Spatz, Susan E. *German Holocaust Literature.* New York: Peter Lang, 1989.

Harris, Frederick J. *Encounters with Darkness: French and German Writers on World War II.* New York: Oxford University Press, 1983.

SHADOWS IN PARADISE
Genre: Novel
Subgenre: Exile fiction
Published: Munich, 1971
Time period: Mid-1940s
Setting: New York and Hollywood

Themes and Issues. Published posthumously, *Shadows in Paradise* was Remarque's final novel and the last in the series of works depicting the experiences of exiles from Nazi Germany. Among the key themes addressed here are the difficulties that refugees faced in escaping from Europe and adjusting to a new life in America.

As such, the novel serves as Remarque's tribute to those exiles who traveled the Via Dolorosa from persecution and imprisonment in Hitler's Germany to internment in France to haven in the United States.

The Plot. The novel recounts the experiences of Robert Ross, a non-Jewish, anti-Nazi German refugee who has just recently arrived in New York following a perilous escape from Europe via Lisbon. Carrying a passport bearing the name of a dead man, he is granted only a temporary residence permit for three months. Soon Ross begins contacting those in the German refugee community who can help him. He encounters several individuals from his past: Kurt Lachmann, an anti-Nazi maimed in the camps, Harry Kahn, a refugee who smuggled people out of France, and Betty Stein, a former literary salon hostess in Berlin. Using skills acquired from hiding out in a Belgian art museum during the German occupation, Ross begins working illegally for two different art dealers. Fearful of being deported and pursued by nightmare visions of the Gestapo (the German secret state police), he yearns for the peaceful stability of a bourgeois existence. Politics seem less important than survival. He forms an intimate relationship with Natasha Petrovna, an attractive French-born fashion model, a relationship that he comes to realize is the most important experience of his life.

As the hired assistant to Silvers, a parasitic art dealer more interested in money than art, Ross travels to Hollywood, where he hawks paintings and serves as a consultant on the Third Reich to a filmmaker. After a short stay there, he returns to New York, where he witnesses the end of the war. The defeat of Nazi Germany brings an end to the gathering of refugees, who now must go their separate ways. Betty Stein, who dreamed only of returning to her beloved Berlin and plotted the Allied advance into the Reich, dies months before final victory. Kahn, like Moller, the German author who lost his audience, commits suicide.

After discussing the matter with Vriesländer,

a well-to-do Jewish refugee who promises to provide him with financial support, Ross decides to return to Germany, not to seek revenge, but to make sure that Nazi crimes do not go unpunished. There he discovers that his former homeland has become an unfamiliar world, and his trip is a "return to indifference, cowardice, and concealed hatred." No one accepts responsibility for the Nazi's actions, and a collective amnesia about the concentration and extermination camps reigns. "Orders were their [the German people's] substitute for conscience."

Analysis. *Shadows in Paradise* was Remarque's final statement on German exile life, a topic he had addressed in several earlier novels. The refugees presented here share a particular bond in that all are dramatically affected by their experiences but react differently. Kurt Lachmann, an anti-Nazi political opponent who was imprisoned, threatened with castration, and left with a permanent limp when his leg was broken, is plagued by recurring nightmares and seeks pleasure only with women who, like himself, have slight physical deformities. Betty Stein, the German Jewish refugee who was imprisoned in the past, attempts to recreate the life she led in Berlin, in which she presided over a literary salon for up-and-coming writers. Harry Kahn, an exile who helped others escape from the Nazis, views Stein's home as a morgue where the living dead reminisce about the dead dead. Vriesländer celebrates his American citizenship by throwing a party and adopting the English name Warwick, which suggests a prominent lineage and at the same time disguises his Jewish roots.

The novel also addresses attitudes in America toward Germans in the 1940s. The main character, Robert Ross, repeatedly encounters antagonism because of his nationality. His girlfriend, Natasha Petrovna, the French-born model descended from Russian parents, abhors the Germans because of what happened to her country after the invasion. Ross informs her that he is not personally responsible since he was interned as an enemy alien in a French camp and had been imprisoned as an enemy of the state in Germany. In another incident the attorney who had been hired to help Ross stay in the United States informs the refugee that he does not work for non-Jewish Germans, whom he views as either Nazis or potential Nazis. Irked at this response, Ross compares this attitude with that of the Nazis who blame the Jews for everything; he states that the Jews left Germany because they were being persecuted and in danger, while non-Jewish Germans who fled did so because they hated Hitler's regime. Remarque also takes a jibe at Hollywood, where German Jewish refugee actors are continually cast as Nazis and where filmmakers portray Hitler's minions as American-style gangsters, as evil incarnate. Ross reminds one such individual

that normal individuals played a key role in the development of mass murder.

As in earlier stories, Remarque's exiles find it difficult to return to their former life. There is no going back, even for those, like Ross, who return to Germany. They confront a society that has dramatically changed in 12 years of Nazi rule; the very language has changed, and once-popular writers are now forgotten or viewed with suspicion or resentment because they lived in exile. Moreover, the exiles themselves have changed. These were experiences that surely Remarque well understood after the war.

SOURCES FOR FURTHER STUDY

Gilbert, Julie. *Opposite Attraction: The Lives of Erich Maria Remarque and Paulette Goddard.* New York: Pantheon Books, 1995.

Taylor, Harley U., Jr. *Erich Maria Remarque: A Literary and Film Biography.* New York: Peter Lang, 1989

Other Works

THE ROAD BACK (1931) AND THREE COMRADES (1938). Published following the gigantic success of *All Quiet on the Western Front, The Road Back* and *Three Comrades* in certain respects serve as quasi sequels to that powerful novel. There is, however, no continuity of characters, since Remarque killed off all the major figures in *All Quiet on the Western Front. The Road Back* and *Three Comrades* both deal with the thorny issue of World War I veterans readjusting to the turbulent world of the Weimar Republic. In the former novel, the main character, Ernst Birkholz, returns from the western front in November 1918 only to find his native Germany embroiled in revolution. His initial optimism about fundamental social change soon gives way to disappointment. He realizes all too keenly that neither he nor his comrades can return to the life they enjoyed before the war or even to the solidarity of the trenches. Unable to adjust to the

new conditions, several of Birkholz's friends suffer personal tragedies and death. The civilian world seems to have little compassion or understanding for the veterans. *Three Comrades,* the first novel Remarque completed after the Nazi takeover of power, addresses the same themes, albeit with different characters and setting.

SPARK OF LIFE (1952) AND A TIME TO LOVE AND A TIME TO DIE (1954). Remarque's final series of works centers upon life in Nazi Germany during the war. Though he could bring no personal experience to bear on these novels, Remarque was profoundly affected by the enormity of Nazi crimes. At the same time that he embarked upon *Spark of Life,* which described life, death, and survival in a German concentration camp, the author began planning a novel focusing largely upon the Reich home front, *A Time to Love and A*

Auschwitz, the Nazi death camp. At Mellern, Remarque's fictional concentration camp, "even a fresh, idealistic SS-man grew bored in time with torturing skeletons. . . . The fact that off and on in the crematorium a live man was burned with the dead was caused more by overwork and the fact that some skeletons hadn't moved for a long time than by evil intent."

Time to Die (1954). In the second book, a German soldier, Ernst Gräber, returns home on leave after serving on the Russian front. There he sees the rubble-filled streets—the result of Allied bombing raids—and discovers the ever-present specter of persecution, where neighbor denounces neighbor in order to satisfy an old vendetta, ideological zeal, or personal gain.

FLOTSAM (1941), ARCH OF TRIUMPH (1945), THE NIGHT IN LISBON (1962), AND SHADOWS IN PARADISE (1971). In this second series of novels, Remarque addresses the trials and tribulations of German refugees forced to flee Hitler's Reich. Though Remarque's situation differed greatly from the individuals he describes in these works, he tried to highlight the sufferings of those who not only were forced to leave their homes because of persecution or political opposition to the Nazis but encountered a world indifferent to their plight. In *Flotsam* the author details the story of a friendship between a Jewish refugee student, Ludwig Kern, and an anti-Nazi German, Josef Steiner, who meet in Austria in 1935. The novel discusses their peregrinations as they travel from one country to another seeking safe haven. Kern falls in love with another Jewish refugee from Germany, Ruth Holland, while Steiner returns to the Reich to visit his dying wife in the hospital. Arrested, Steiner makes a deal with his Nazi adversary, Steinbrenner, who allows him to attend to his wife. Following her death, he plunges out of the hospital window, taking Steinbrenner with him. In Paris, Ruth and Ludwig procure tickets to Mexico, where they hope to begin a new life. In his second exile novel, *Arch of Triumph,* Remarque depicts the unfolding love story in Paris between a German refugee physician, Dr. Ravic (born Ludwig Fresenburg), and Joan Madou, an actress, perhaps modeled on Marlene Dietrich. Following Joan's tragic death and the outbreak of World War II, Ravic is interned by French authorities and later takes revenge upon the SS officer who tortured him and murdered his wife. Completing the series of exile novels are *The Night in Lisbon* and *Shadows in Paradise,* the former detailing the experiences of two German refugees hoping to leave Europe for the security of the United States and the latter addressing refugee life in America.

Resources

There are several major repositories of documents relating to Erich Maria Remarque and his works scattered throughout the world. Below are several of the most prominent archives.

Erich Maria Remarque and Paulette Goddard Papers and Library. Located at Fales Library, New York University, this collection is largely made up of materials donated in 1990 to NYU by the author's widow, Paulette Goddard. It consists of more than 62,000 pages of diaries, original manuscripts, letters, photographs, and personal effects. In addition, the collection contains some 3,000 works from Remarque's own library. It serves as the world's leading repository of the author's work and an essential archival stop for scholars in the field (www.nyu.edu/library/bobst/research/fales/exhibits/remarque/documents/bio.html). Also located at NYU is the Remarque Institute, an organization created in 1995 through a large bequest from Paulette Goddard to foster the "study and discussion of Europe, and to encourage and facilitate communication between Americans and Europeans."

Erich Maria Remarque Peace Center. Founded in 1989 by the city of Osnabrück, Germany, and affiliated with the University of Osnabrück, the center houses a major archive dedicated to the study of the author's work, as well as the Erich Maria Remarque

Gesellschaft, a literary organization that strives to "promote and support humanistic culture, art, sciences, and research through cultivating Erich Maria Remarque's heritage and range of thought." The archive contains various editions of his novels, in addition to a microfilm copy of much of the original materials housed at New York University. Each year the Remarque Gesellschaft publishes the *Remarque Jahrbuch,* a scholarly yearbook dedicated to the author's literary legacy. In addition, the center presents the Erich Maria Remarque Peace Award to individuals whose work fosters peace. The center's Web site contains information in German and English on the author and his work (www.remarque.uos.de).

Marlene Dietrich Collection Berlin. Created in 1993 by the state of Berlin and run by the Filmmuseum Berlin, the collection contains tens of thousands of items from the late actress's personal estate, including her costumes, clothing, scripts, and correspondence with many prominent figures, including Erich Maria Remarque. Information on the collection can be accessed through the organization's Web site, though one must be able to read German to use it (www.filmmuseum-berlin.de/samml/sa_cont10.htm).

STEVEN LUCKERT

Jean Rhys

BORN: August 24, 1890, Roseau, Dominica, West Indies
DIED: May 14, 1979, Exeter, England
IDENTIFICATION: Postcolonial, postmodernist writer whose novels and short stories often feature female protagonists isolated from the surrounding society.

SIGNIFICANCE: In 1954 Jean Rhys wrote, "I must write. If I stop writing my life will have been an abject failure. . . . I will not have earned death." The author of many short stories and novels, of which *Wide Sargasso Sea* is perhaps best known, Rhys, who wrote throughout her long life, was known as a modernist writer and often grouped with Joseph Conrad and T. S. Eliot. Her themes frequently involve isolation from a community, the sense of things falling apart, and investigations of dependence and loss. Often set in metropolitan locations, her stories evince a concern for subjectivity and employ an almost poetic language, rich in irony and subtle in diction.

The Writer's Life

Born Ella Rees Williams to a Dominican Creole mother and a Welsh-born doctor in Roseau, on the Leeward Island of Dominica in the West Indies, Jean Rhys experienced concerns involving race and colonization from early in her life. Rhys's experiences as a white Creole woman, both in the Caribbean and in England, deeply influenced her life and writing. As a white girl in a predominantly black community, Rhys often felt socially and intellectually isolated. As a child she loved literature and longed to visit the seemingly exotic places about which she read. Only later in life would she realize that she lived in a wildly exotic place for much of her childhood.

This photograph, taken on the Leeward Island of Dominica in the West Indies sometime before 1895, shows Rhys as a toddler. The adults in the photograph are unidentified.

A Caribbean Setting. Although Rhys's attitude to her birthplace remained ambivalent throughout her life, the Caribbean shaped her sensibility. She remained nostalgic for the emotional vitality of its peoples, and the conflict between its beauty and its violent history became enmeshed in the tensions of her own often fraught personality. Even when Europe was Rhys's home, the West Indies was a part of her literary consciousness and her feelings of self-identification. She explored her own background in a search for meaning and rootedness. Details of this exploration would mark most of her writing.

Rhys's Dominican background played a part in both her longer fiction, including *Voyage in the Dark,* and in short stories, such as "The Day They Burned the Books." Dominica is the most rugged of the Caribbean islands. Despite being only 29 miles long, the island's peaks rise to more than 5,000 feet. The violent contrasts between dense vegetation, deep gorges, waterfalls, and stretches of arid wasteland are totally unlike the atmosphere that Rhys was presented with upon her arrival in Britain. The bizarre extremes of the landscape resonate in *Wide Sargasso Sea,* in which Rochester's attitude toward beauty is to mistrust its lushness.

Childhood. Rhys identified with the African-based community in her childhood and indeed throughout her life, although she came to realize that her world could never align itself with that of her nursemaid, Meta, and other black mentors. She envied the vitality of this community. In her writing she often contrasts the sterility of the white world with the richness and splendor of black life. Themes of attempted friendship with black girls recur in her work, an obvious example being the figures of Tia and Christophine in *Wide Sargasso Sea,* but Anna Morgan in *Voyage in the Dark* also attempts to find a friend among the blacks.

Rhys's early life paralleled that of other post-colonial writers who felt themselves betrayed by the reality of Britain. Rhys would not find a social niche in England until she was in her seventies. Shaped by her instinctive drives and created out of the struggle to comprehend her own isolated predicament, she and her writing were both obstinately unconventional. In part, this unwillingness to conform prevented her work from receiving due recognition for much of her lifetime.

The Fledgling Artist. In 1907 Rhys's father sent the 17-year-old to school in England. Rhys would return to her home again only once, in 1936. She attended the Perse School in Cambridge (1907–1908), and the Royal Academy of Dramatic Art in London (1909). Forced to abandon her studies when her father died, Rhys turned to her artistic skills, including dancing as a chorus girl with a touring musical company during 1909 and 1910. While she was receiving a small allowance from a former lover, Rhys also ghostwrote a nonfiction book about furniture. During World War I she volunteered for the war effort, first serving as a volunteer in a soldiers' canteen and later working for a year in a pension office.

Passion drove Rhys, whether in her everyday life or in her writing. In 1919 she went to Holland and married the French-Dutch journalist and songwriter John Lenglet. From 1920 to 1922, they lived in Budapest and then moved on to Paris. By 1927 they had settled in England. They had two children, a son who died in infancy and a daughter. During this period Rhys began writing under the patronage of the English writer Ford Madox Ford, whom she met in Paris. When her husband was sentenced to prison for illegal financial transactions, Rhys began an affair with Ford. Ultimately, the affair ended bitterly, and Rhys and her husband were divorced.

Growing Popularity. From this point forward, Rhys lived a painful and often lonely life. In 1934 she married Leslie Tilden Smith, who

FILMS BASED ON RHYS'S STORIES

1959 *Good Morning, Midnight* (BBC)

1981 *Quartet*

1993 *Wide Sargasso Sea*

In this posed studio shot, taken by professional photographer Pearl Freeman, a young Rhys stares pensively into the camera.

HIGHLIGHTS IN RHYS'S LIFE

1890   Ella Rees Williams is born on August 24, 1890, in Dominica, West Indies.

1907–1908 Rhys attends the Perse School, Cambridge.

1909–1910 Tours as a chorus girl.

1919   Marries John Lenglet and moves to Paris; gives birth on December 29 to a son, who dies three weeks later.

1922   Meets the English author Ford Madox Ford.

1923–1924 Rhys's husband is imprisoned for illegal financial transactions; Rhys begins an affair with Ford.

1927   *The Left Bank and Other Stories* is published; the writer adopts the pen name Jean Rhys.

1929   *Quartet: A Novel* is published.

1932   Rhys divorces Lenglet.

1934   Marries Leslie Tilden Smith; publishes *Voyage in the Dark*.

1939   Publishes *Good Morning, Midnight*.

1947   Marries Max Hamer.

1957–1966 Works on *Wide Sargasso Sea*.

1966   *Wide Sargasso Sea* is published.

1979   Rhys dies in Exeter, England, on May 14; *Smile Please: An Unfinished Autobiography* is posthumously published.

died in 1945. Two years later she married Max Hamer, who had served a prison term. He died in 1966. Rhys continued her writing, but from 1939 to 1957, she lived almost entirely outside public attention. During most of this period, she lived in the west country of Great Britain, often in great poverty. In 1959 her novel *Good Morning, Midnight* was adapted by her close friend, the Dutch-born actress and screenwriter Selma Vaz Dias, for the BBC (British Broadcasting Corporation). Encouraged by Francis Wyndham, Rhys started to write again, and her short stories were published in the *London Magazine* and in *Art and Letters*. Rhys continued to live alone in her primitive Devon cottage at Cheriton Fitzpaine, drinking heavily but still writing. After learning of the great public interest generated by radio broadcasts of

This still from the 1993 film adaptation of *Wide Sargasso Sea,* the wildly successful comeback novel that draws on Rhys's own experiences growing up in the Caribbean, reflects the isolation felt by Antoinette, played by actress Karina Lombard. "I often wonder who I am and where is my country and where do I belong and why was I ever born at all," Rhys wrote.

her work, Rhys recommitted herself to writing. She spent the years 1957 through 1966 working on her masterpiece, *Wide Sargasso Sea.*

The Turning Point. Published in 1966, this novel derived from the author's early life. Jean Rhys's great-grandfather, John Potter Lockhart, acquired a plantation in Dominica in 1824. After his death in 1837, his widow was left to run the estate. The riots in 1844 following emancipation led to the destruction of the estate and the burning of the house. Rhys visited the plantation and was affected by the experience. An awareness of this incident may help to explain some of the more ambiguous attitudes in *Wide Sargasso Sea,* such as Antoinette's caustic remarks to Christophine and Tia about their blackness. Rhys's own background, as well as Antoinette's, was that of the former slave-owning Creole community.

Last Years. Rhys's final years brought fame and freedom from financial anxiety but no work of similar importance. She published a collection of new short stories, *Sleep It Off Lady,* and worked on her autobiography, unfinished at her death but published posthumously as *Smile Please: An Unfinished Autobiography*

HERE LIE BURIED THE ASHES
OF MY BELOVED MOTHER
JEAN RHYS, C.B.E., NOVELIST
(ELLA GWENDOLEN HAMER)
BORN
DOMINICA AUGUST 24TH 1890
DIED
EXETER MAY 14TH 1979.
"GOOD MORNING MIDNIGHT."

Tombstone in an English cemetery erected by Rhys's daughter to mark her mother's gravesite. The surname "Hamer" is the name of Rhys's third husband and her married name at the time of her death.

(1979). Her letters were published in 1984 in England, edited by Francis Wyndham and Diana Melly. These letters helped establish Rhys's literary image: a West Indies–born writer, self-destructive and alcoholic, with a clear familiarity with the seedy side of life. Rhys called herself "a doormat in a world of boots."

Appropriately, her fiction deals with the theme of the helpless female, victimized by her dependence on a man for support and protection.

During her career Rhys received many awards, including the W. H. Smith Award, the Royal Society of Literature Award, and an Arts Council Bursary. She died on May 14, 1979, in Exeter.

The Writer's Work

In all of her work, critics generally assumed that Rhys created heroines with a personal makeup very similar to her own. Rhys admitted as much; she particularly attempted to portray the unique situations of women isolated and relying on their own strength to endure difficulty. Critics (mostly English) in the early years of Rhys's career also assumed that she was "nonintellectual" because they thought she did not make many allusions to other texts. However, it turned out that, in fact, Rhys made many literary allusions—to French texts with which the English critics were unfamiliar.

Placing Rhys's Work. In studying the writings of Jean Rhys, questions of identity frequently surface, both in relation to Rhys herself and in relation to her heroines. The critic Veronica Marie Gregg writes, "There seems to be a wide range of interpretive options for an analysis of Jean Rhys's writing: West Indian, Third World, British, Euro-American, European, feminist, postcolonial. Regardless of the theoretical models used, many critiques take for granted, or as a point of departure, a psychobiography of the writer herself: her birth in the West Indies, her peripatetic life, her being a British or colonial woman writer, or a writer who does not seem to fit anywhere." Critics formed a theory that Rhys's work grew out of a composite heroine and that Rhys dealt with the same woman at different stages of her career. This approach led the critical consensus to create a "Jean Rhys woman."

French actress Isabelle Adjani (center) appeared as the character Marya Zelli in the 1981 British film *Quartet,* based on Rhys's novel of the same name. The well-received film was nominated for the Golden Palm at the 1981 Cannes Film Festival, where Adjani won the award for best actress.

Colonial Context. Rhys's personal situation suggests that she had greater insight than others into inequities in European social structures. Teresa F. O'Conner writes that the cultural context of Rhys's novels is a crucial setting. However, she writes, "when the room is all that one of Rhys's heroines has, one knows that she has reached the limit of destitution, isolation, and hopelessness . . . the causes for that finale are not simply the result of a passive and self-destructive personality. They are social and historical as well." The room essentially has the same symbolic meaning for all of Rhys's heroines. Another common symbol for the heroines of Rhys's novels is clothing, a symbol closely associated with identity. Gregg points to the incident in *Wide Sargasso Sea* when Antoinette and Tia get into a fight over three pennies and Tia subsequently steals Antoinette's dress. Similarly, in *Voyage in the Dark* and *Good Morning,*

The despair, dejection, and hopelessness on the face of this Spanish woman sitting alone in a small room, having been made homeless by the Spanish Civil War, embodies the disorientation and despair of Sasha Jansen, Rhys's protagonist in *Good Morning, Midnight.*

This woman, homeless and alone on the road, in French artist Jacques Dumont's painting *Poor Woman with the Children* (Pushkin Museum of Fine Arts, Moscow), typifies the theme Rhys dealt with in her writings: a helpless female who is victimized by her need to depend on a man for support and protection.

It is very difficult to pin down the specific influences and inspirations that underlie the novels and stories of Jean Rhys—apart, that is, from her use of the well-remembered characteristics of the lush Caribbean of her birth and the very free hand with which she transposed autobiographical details to her fiction. Indeed, she once famously told an interviewer that she considered herself neither West Indian ("It was such a long time ago when I left") nor English ("I'm not, I'm not!") and certainly not French. Only in *Wide Sargasso Sea* can one detect what might fairly be called a Brontë connection. Rhys brilliantly imagined the possibility of another side to *Jane Eyre,* and in doing so she produced not only a remarkable deconstruction of Charlotte Brontë's famed novel but also a damning history of European colonialism in the Caribbean.

From the time she was born until she was 17 and left for schooling in England, Rhys lived in the Caribbean, surrounded by rampant, colorful, abundant nature. This photograph shows a river in a valley covered with lush foliage on the island of Dominica. Seeing such beautiful scenes as a part of daily life formed deeply imprinted memories that reappear throughout Rhys's writings.

Midnight, dress becomes an important symbol. For Anna in *Voyage in the Dark,* clothing represents a way to change her social status.

Language. In her novels Rhys uses languages other than English. Often she employs language as a vehicle through which the powerful maintain control. Rhys constructs her own vocabulary in an effort to get past the clichés of the English language and to reject much of the language of the British Empire and all that it symbolizes for her, including such notions as colonialism, class, bourgeois values, and morality. Especially in her novels the reader encounters language structures that are frequently fragmented, the words weaving and following associations before circling back for certain events and phrases.

Rhys also uses multiple voices in her writing, including inner dialogue, indirect speech, letters, and dreams. She also utilizes echoes of conversations, songs, poetry, and quotes from books, letters, and prayers. By using this type of narrative voice, Rhys is able to reshape, resist, and transform language through her rejection of what already exists. This device is particularly evident in *Wide Sargasso Sea,* which is a story based on characters in Charlotte Brontë's *Jane Eyre.*

Rhys was haunted by the figure of the first Mrs. Rochester, the mad wife in *Jane Eyre,* whom readers know only through Rochester's

LONG FICTION	SHORT FICTION	AUTOBIOGRAPHY
1929 Quartet (originally published as Postures in 1928)	1927 The Left Bank and Other Stories	1979 Smile Please: An Unfinished Autobiography
1931 After Leaving Mr. Mackenzie	1968 Tigers Are Better-Looking (including a selection from the Left Bank)	
1934 Voyage in the Dark		
1939 Good Morning, Midnight	1976 Sleep It Off Lady	
1966 Wide Sargasso Sea		
1975 My Day		

biased descriptions. She is defined for readers purely as a foreigner, a victim, entirely defined by and in the power of a man, her white English husband, Rochester. Rhys wanted to change this perception, to give Mrs. Rochester a voice. *Wide Sargasso Sea* breaks away from the nineteenth-century tradition by taking the viewpoint of the other woman and by centering the narrative on this woman about whom so little is known. While some writers would be intimidated at the idea of supplementing the work of a great writer such as Charlotte Brontë, Rhys centers her attention on what has not been said or on what she thinks has been told falsely.

Anyone who has read *Jane Eyre* knows how *Wide Sargasso Sea* will end. However, Rhys develops the pain and isolation as Antoinette hurtles toward her inevitable demise. Especially in *Wide Sargasso Sea*, Rhys shows that "the other" can become a central and essential part of literature. By taking what has been written, ignoring the existing guidelines and structures, and creating her own rules of language and format, Rhys has been able to transform a character perceived as a victim into a powerful figure.

Modernist Writing. While Rhys's fiction gives the appearance of being simplicity itself, it is not. Yet her elusiveness is not in the tradition established by the writers Gertrude Stein, Djuna Barnes, James Joyce, and Virginia Woolf. It is interesting to note that Rhys is perpetually ignored by critics of the experimental even though she is also ignored by critics of realism, because she does not fit easily into a realistic tradition either. Her closest modernist counterpart is the American writer Ernest Hemingway both mistrust language, both critique its inadequacies even as they use it, and both, at their best, invent characters who are just barely hanging on, trying to survive to the next day, trying to numb themselves. Unlike Hemingway, Rhys does not employ romantic trappings. The closest she comes to such devices is in *Good Morning, Midnight* (1939), which contains a character who is a gigolo not far removed from Hemingway's Brett Ashley in *The Sun Also Rises*.

BIBLIOGRAPHY

Angiers, Carole. *Jean Rhys: A Life and Work*. Boston: Little, Brown, 1990.

Gregg, Veronica Marie. *Jean Rhys's Historical Imagination: Reading and Writing the Creole*. Chapel Hill: University of North Carolina Press, 1995.

Harrison, Nancy R. *Jean Rhys and the Novel as Women's Text*. Chapel Hill: University of North Carolina Press, 1988.

Maurel, Sylvie. *Jean Rhys*. New York: St. Martin's Press, 1998.

O'Conner, Teresa F. *Jean Rhys: The West Indian Novels*. New York: New York University Press, 1988.

Savory, Elaine. *Jean Rhys*. New York: Cambridge University Press, 1998.

Sternlicht, Stanley. *Jean Rhys*. New York: Prentice Hall, 1997.

Thomas, Sue. *The Worlding of Jean Rhys*. Greenwood, CT: Greenwood Press, 1999.

Understanding and "Positioning" the Works of Jean Rhys

Critics struggle over where exactly to place Jean Rhys in the literary canon. Her novels, particularly *Wide Sargasso Sea,* are taught in courses in women's literature, world literature, European literature, and West Indian literature, to name only a few. Rhys does not help the situation in two important ways: her own ethnicity is a diverse mix of Creole and European influences, and her works vary considerably in theme and locale.

In short, Rhys acquires outsider status in a variety of settings. Viewing Rhys as a third world writer as well as a woman in exile in Paris may help readers better understand her position there. Isolated from women and taken up by men as a protégée or mistress, Rhys's experience of exile was different, by virtue of her colonial background, from that of someone like the American writer Gertrude Stein and, by virtue of her sex, from that of someone like the Jamaica-born American writer Claude McKay. She married three times and bore two children; she suffered from illness, poverty, and dependence on alcohol. In these facts one finds the traces of social forces that denied poor women proper medical and child care and denied unmarried women livelihoods and respectability.

Still, the categorization of Rhys's work is made more difficult by the "double homelessness" that infects her characters and indeed the author herself. An individual's identity is formed in a home environment by interaction with a family and within a particular culture. Yet the characters in Rhys's early novels lack both homes and homelands. Circumstances and their own actions have isolated them from families, husbands, and friends. The driving theme becomes the restless search of these women to know themselves in in-between spaces, both physical and psychological.

Thus, reacting to more complexity than they are comfortable with, many scholars position Rhys on the basis of the ethnic nuance in her writing—but again, Rhys's attitude varies considerably from work to work. A West Indian critic, Wally Look Lai, urges critics to categorize *Wide Sargasso Sea* with West Indian literature: "It is not that [this novel] provides a mere background to the theme of rejected womanhood, but rather that the theme of rejected womanhood is utilized symbolically in order to make an artistic statement about West Indian society, and about an aspect of the West Indian experience."

Critics who are fond of this perspective emphasize Rhys's use of detailed descriptions of place and weather; casual references to the color of the sky and degrees of light, heat, or shade; allusions to the scents and tints of flowers; and observations of the natives' behavior. Rhys joins physical descriptions of place with linguistic variations to capture the ethnic diversity of the West Indies. Characters use language that indicates their English, French, African, or white West Indian descent. The language in *Wide Sargasso Sea*, in particular, has an authentic ring to a West Indian's ear and evokes, in a way no didactic account can, the whole social spectrum in the West Indies.

Rhys, in the later years of her life, shown here at her cottage in Cheriton Fitzpaine in Devon, England.

Whatever the setting, however, Rhys seems to maintain consistent patterns of imagery. In *Wide Sargasso Sea* she contrasts lush tropical sensuality with cold English calculation. Like the poet Sylvia Plath, Rhys uses her life experiences—the pain, the rawness, and the wounds—as the material upon which she draws to write her fiction. In fact, many of her heroines have been made up of fragments of her own self. Why then do her heroines do nothing to get out of their situations?

A significant debate has centered on the idea of the helpless victim in Rhys's writing. Indeed, Rhys allows Antoinette to rise above her situation by seeking final revenge on Rochester and gaining back her independence, her sanity, and her life. Given this perspective, it is not surprising that Rhys's work has recently gained popularity as feminist literature. In the 1970s, when she was still alive, feminism centered on sexual oppression and excluded Jean Rhys's literature. What the feminists of the seventies did not realize was that Rhys was years ahead of them. While they centered solely on what they regarded as sexual oppression, Rhys questioned economic, racial, class, and colonial oppression, too. Only since the 1980s has Rhys's work become widely recognized as a valuable addition to feminist literature.

V. S. Naipaul, however, has suggested that Rhys be read in terms of colonial origins. In fact, her Caribbean origins long went largely unmentioned. The publication of *Wide Sargasso Sea* coincided with the recognition of West Indian literature as a valuable addition to world literature. Naipaul's suggestion having been widely seconded, Rhys's work has been enthusiastically welcomed in the world of postcolonial literature.

Such disparity in approach to a novelist's work has not precluded its appeal to a wide cross section of readers, and therein lies Rhys's greatest strength. It is also because of this strength that her writing has become an inviting subject for discussion and analysis in literature courses.

Reader's Guide to Major Works

GOOD MORNING, MIDNIGHT

Genre: Postmodernist novel
Subgenre: Postcolonial, feminist fiction
Published: 1939
Time period: Late 1930s
Setting: Paris, France

Themes and Issues. *Good Morning, Midnight* reads as if one were listening to someone rambling on, with little or no context provided. Rhys's method underlying this approach, which originates in character, is to make all things (events, objects, people) equal or at least present them to the reader as equal. Where the narrator is going to go for her next drink is just as significant as the death of her baby: all experiences exist in the same reality. In fact, at one point the narrator's friend tells her that things do not all exist on the same plane, but indeed, for this character they do, as they do for the method of ordering and narrative information in the novel.

The Plot. *Good Morning, Midnight* is about Sasha Jansen, a down-and-out woman renting a room in Paris in the late 1930s, a place she can afford only because a friend has given her the money for it. At some ill-defined point in her life, she had what was apparently a small inheritance, though the reader is not told who died in order to provide it. Several years earlier, Sasha lived in Paris with her lover, Enno, the father of her only child (who died a short time after birth). With Sasha constantly wondering where she will get her next drink, one might guess that she is an alcoholic (one might also guess any number of other things), but her alcoholism is not explained. She lives next door to a man of whom she is terrified, though the reader is never told why. Most of the novel consists of disjointed episodes from both her present and her past—failed loves, failed jobs. Late in the novel the reader finds out she is a writer.

Rhys uses a modified stream-of-consciousness technique to portray the consciousness of an aging woman, Sasha Jansen. Sasha has returned to Paris, where she reviews her happiest and most desperate moments of life. "She must cry so that others may be able to laugh the more heartily." When she is picked up by a young man, she renews her relationship with the society outside. *Good Morning, Midnight* is a brilliant evocation of psychic disorientation and despair. The heroine, Sasha, remembers a life of love and defeat and faces the ultimate darkness suggested by the novel's title. Told as a first-person narrative alternating between the past tense and the continuous present, *Good Morning, Midnight* is a technical tour de force.

Analysis. *Good Morning, Midnight* is deliberately disjointed in nature. Time and causal relationships, like everything else in the novel, are treated as reflective of character, and for Sasha Jansen (whose real name is not even Sasha, though this fact, buried in an aside of sorts, seems to have eluded most of Rhys's critics), time also exists on a single plane. Though Sasha does not differentiate between what happens in the present and what happened 15 years earlier, how the reader might react would be affected if time sequences and relationships were clearer. In Sasha's world, however, events and experiences repeat themselves, and so the difference between what happened between Sasha and a lover 15 years ago is, for her, only another manifestation of what is happening now. Therefore, "this happened and then that," but the "this" and the "that" do not follow a causal pattern. Is there a relationship encompassing her father (mentioned once in a dream), her lover Enno (the gigolo lover in the present), and the menacing figure who lives in the room next door and with whom she winds up in bed on the novel's last page? Probably or maybe or perhaps simply no. Sasha makes no connections, and any connections the reader

Max Ernst's 1912 self-portrait (Wilhelm Hack Museum, Ludwigshafen, Germany) captures the disjointed single-plane mind-set of Rhys's narrator Sasha Jansen in *Good Morning, Midnight.* The painting evokes Sasha's method of telling her story: backward and forward, present and past, all in the now.

might try to make are impeded by the method Rhys uses. What is not available to Sasha is not made available to the reader. In short, the reader is forced to read the novel the way that Sasha experiences things: fragmentedly, elliptically, confusedly.

The act of reading Jean Rhys's *Good Morning, Midnight* and what one may do afterward with what one has read are two very different things. Rhys's critics have weighed in with a variety of opinions on her technique—from squeezing her into the role of a minor modernist to elevating her to the status of an unheralded feminist. The critics, as usual, in their attempts at interpretation largely undermine the nature of the writer's art and miss what the experience of reading is.

SOURCES FOR FURTHER STUDY

Emery, Mary Lou. *Jean Rhys at "World's End": Novels of Colonial and Sexual Exile.* Austin: University of Texas Press, 1990.

Gregg, Veronica Marie. *Jean Rhys's Historical Imagination: Reading and Writing the Creole.* Chapel Hill: University of North Carolina Press, 1995.

Le Gallez, Paula. *The Rhys Woman.* Hampshire, UK: Macmillan, 1990.

Nebeker, Helen. *Jean Rhys, Woman in Passage: A Critical Study of the Novels of Jean Rhys.* St. Albans, VT: Eden Press Women's Publications, 1981.

WIDE SARGASSO SEA

Genre: Modernist novel
Subgenre: Postcolonial, Caribbean fiction
Published: 1966
Time period: Late nineteenth century
Setting: Caribbean, Great Britain

Themes and Issues. In writing the novel *Wide Sargasso Sea,* it was the ambition of Jean Rhys to create a history and understanding of the character Bertha Rochester, the mad wife of Mr. Rochester in Charlotte Brontë's *Jane Eyre.* In order to do so, Rhys set herself up to appropriate Brontë's story, the consciousness of a woman (Bertha) who goes insane, and the perspective of an English gentleman (Rochester). It took Rhys nine years to create these charac-ters and a story that empathetically provided a culturally accurate defense for both Bertha and Rochester. The time commitment in itself is evidence that Rhys was dedicated to a responsible creation of this story. In *Wide Sargasso Sea,* Rhys focuses on the differences between people who come from various places. The symbolism of the title suggests the barriers, such as bodies of water, that separate people. The novel is told from the perspective of Bertha in the first and last sections and from the perspective of Rochester in the middle section. Rhys does not depict either character as a hero or villain but rather focuses on the complexity of each and the dynamics of their relationship and why it failed them both.

The Plot. Divided into three sections, *Wide Sargasso Sea* begins with Antoinette's narrative of her childhood and homeland. The second section is told primarily from the point of view of Antoinette's husband, Rochester (who is not named in the novel). The third section consists of Antoinette's reaction to England and her ultimate descent into madness.

Existing as a white Creole woman in post-Emancipation West Indian society, Antoinette Cosway lives a life of "in-betweenness." It is this sense of in-betweenness, of belonging to neither culture, that is the primary factor driving Antoinette into madness. While she is able to move between black and white cultures, she is also scorned by those cultures. Antoinette is "neither English and rich, nor native and part of the community of slaves freed by the Emancipation Act," and she "must navigate her way through these treacherous landscapes of Creole and English identity." She remembers that even Tia, an early childhood friend with whom she used to walk to school, would harass her. Tia would do so because Antoinette's family, once wealthy slave owners, had become just as poor as many of the black families living nearby. Antoinette says that there are "plenty white people in Jamaica. Real white people, they got gold money. They didn't look at us, nobody see them come near us." It seems that Antoinette cannot win. She is attacked for being white, yet in the same paragraph, she is attacked for not being white enough. Tia later attacks Antoinette again when, after her house has been burned to the ground, she tries to turn to Tia for comfort. As she runs to Tia, wishing to "be like her," she gets hit in the face with a rock that Tia throws at her. Antoinette says, "we stared at each other, blood on my face, tears on hers. It was as if I saw myself. Like in a looking glass."

Giacomo Balla's 1905 oil-on-canvas painting *Mad Woman* evokes the pain, heartbreak, and descent into insanity of Rhys's Antoinette in *Wide Sargasso Sea.* The colorful brightness at the subject's back as she faces and prepares to enter a gray room reflects the dichotomy Antoinette faces in being unable to be understood by either her black or her white world.

The image of the looking glass is important here because it symbolizes Antoinette's need to find her "other" self, her identity. Her inability to reach through to the other side of the mirror symbolizes her inability to find and grasp that other self. This effort of self-discovery makes up the rest of the action of the novel.

The final and ultimate stripping away of Antoinette's identity is done when Rochester moves her and himself to England. By taking her away from her homeland, Rochester has taken her even further away from her identity as a West Indian woman. He has taken away any chance that she might have in trying to establish an identity. Once in England, Antoinette is seen as a madwoman. She no longer envisions England as a fantasy. Now she describes it as a "cardboard world where everything is colored brown or dark red or yellow that has no light in it." Antoinette reflects a great deal during the short segment of the book that covers her stay in England. As she reflects, she remembers a looking glass she used to have—how better to suggest the character's retreat within herself.

Rhys suggests that Antoinette will be saved from this "living death" in the last paragraph of the novel. After having a dream in which she sees herself burning Rochester's mansion, Antoinette takes a candle from her room and walks down the hall. It is suggested that through burning down the mansion, Antoinette will regain the power that she has lost to Rochester. The flames will have purifying effects. It is also suggested that she will finally establish an identity for herself, even if it is through death. In the dream in which she burns down the mansion, Antoinette also sees Tia standing near a pool, beckoning Antoinette to join her.

The pool's significance is similar to that of the looking glass, the reflection being Antoinette's identity. The difference here is that this looking glass, the pool, is permeable. There is no hard cold glass to stop her from joining identities, and her ability to get to the other side of the reflection symbolizes her ultimate "completion" of herself. By jumping into the pool, she will finally be able to merge the colonial blackness and Creole whiteness that have torn her apart and driven her to madness.

Analysis. Antoinette's disillusionment in her relationships with her mother and her husband, her lack of a strong connection with Christophine and Tia, and her inability to be completely understood by either the white culture or the black culture leave her a woman without an identity, a woman with no path open to her save madness. Rhys's depiction of the effects of colonialism in the West Indies is a dark one. Antoinette's life is a picture of heartbreak, destruction, and insanity in which there can be no in-betweens. Rhys is able, however, to allow her character to transcend the bounds of the repetitious entrapment that characterizes so many stories of the Caribbean and to offer her liberation.

Rhys divides the novel's narration between Rochester and Antoinette and in so doing avoids suppressing alternative voices—a criticism she voiced about Brontë's text. Rochester, who is never named in the novel, is not portrayed as an evil tyrant but as a proud and bigoted younger brother betrayed by his family into a loveless marriage. His double standard with regard to the former slaves and Antoinette's family involvement with them is exposed when he chooses to sleep with the maid, Amelie. This action shows that he is guilty of the promiscuous behavior and the attraction to the black community of which he had accused and upbraided Antoinette. The couple's brief days of happiness at Granbois are halted by Rochester's willingness to believe the worst of Antoinette.

Rhys "negotiates" with Brontë's novel. Since *Jane Eyre* is part of the received canon, the merging of Antoinette's fate into that of Bertha's is inevitable; still, Rhys allows the reader to interpret the fate of Antoinette differently by leaving the ending open. Antoinette dreams of the fire and leaps to her death, but the novel ends with her resolution to act rather than with a description of her death or with an exact repetition of Brontë's words. Thus, the possibility of a different fate for Rhys's character is left intact. One might say that the more recent text can be said to extend the older's possibilities.

When *Wide Sargasso Sea* was released as a film in 1993, it received a great deal of acclaim. The film works hard to convey the climate in which it takes place. The island is sunny and humid, the nights warm and damp, and sweat is allowed to glisten on the skin of the actors, instead of their being mopped up and dusted down by the makeup crew. A hothouse atmosphere permeates every scene, creating an unhealthy climate in which young love is perverted, promises become lies, and jealousy becomes the strongest emotion. Some film critics consider the movie a minor masterpiece.

SOURCES FOR FURTHER STUDY

Adjarian, M. M. "Between and Beyond Boundaries in *Wide Sargasso Sea*." *College Literature* 22 (Feb. 1995).

Carr, Helen. *Jean Rhys*. Plymouth, UK: Northcote House, 1996.

Ciolkowski, Laura E. "Navigating the Wide Sargasso Sea: Colonial History, English Fiction, and British Empire." *Twentieth Century Literature* 43 (1997).

Gardiner, Judith K. *Rhys, Stead, Lessing and the Politics of Empathy*. Indianapolis: Indiana University Press, 1989.

Hearne, John. "*The Wide Sargasso Sea*: A West Indian Reflection." *Cornhill Magazine* 180 (1974): 323–333.

James, Selma. *The Ladies and the Mammies: Jane Austen and Jean Rhys*. Bristol, UK: Falling Wall Press, 1983.

Nixon, Nicola. "*Wide Sargasso Sea* and Jean Rhys's Interrogation of the 'Nature Wholly Alien' in *Jane Eyre*." *Essays in Literature* 21, no. 2 (Fall 1994): 267–284.

Staley, Thomas F. *Jean Rhys: A Critical Study*. London: Macmillan, 1979.

Other Works

THE LEFT BANK AND OTHER STORIES (1927). It was with the publication of this, her first collection of short fiction, that the writer took the pen name Jean Rhys. Rhys's short fiction exhibits a remarkable variety of themes. A significant number of stories recall her childhood in the Caribbean and range from a girl's cruel sexual awakening ("Goodbye Marcus, Goodbye Rose") to incisive sketches of the narrowness of small-island life ("The Day They Burned the Books"). Others, such as "Vienne," reflect Rhys's restless bohemian life in Europe. In "Let Them Call It Jazz," Rhys assumes the personality of Selina, a black West Indian in London whose struggles parallel her own. However, although Rhys declared, "I have only ever written about myself," it is important that her life and her writing not be confused.

VOYAGE IN THE DARK (1934). Rhys's third published but first written novel, *Voyage in the Dark,* is her most autobiographical work of fiction. Its heroine, Anna Morgan, aged 19, has come to England from Dominica. The novel opens with a compelling evocation of the Caribbean, its colors, sights, smells, and warmth. As the novel recounts Anna's attempt to come to terms with her new life, the inner narrative traces a remembered life in the Caribbean. In this first novel Rhys's protagonist is the first in a line of mistreated, unlucky female characters. The young chorus girl Anna places herself in the hands of her older lover, has an abortion, and becomes the passive victim of other men and women.

QUARTET: A NOVEL (1929). Originally published in 1928 as *Postures,* Rhys's first novel was released widely the following year with the title *Quartet.* While it lacks the confidence of her later work, in the character of Marya Zelli *Quartet* introduced what was to become the recognizable Rhys heroine—sensitive, sexually attractive, and vulnerable, with a tendency to self-defeat. It also shows Rhys's stylistic control in moving within characters and in observing them objectively, without irony. *Quartet* is Rhys's version of a classic tale, that of the fate of an innocent, helpless female protagonist

Wilson Bigaud's twentieth-century painting *"Ra-Ra" Haitian Carnival Scene,* with its depiction of a colorful Caribbean celebration, reflects the opening of Rhys's novel *Voyage in the Dark.*

caught in a sexual liaison whose stakes and motives completely escape her. The book is widely regarded as an account of Rhys's affair with Ford Madox Ford.

AFTER LEAVING MR. MACKENZIE

(1931). In *After Leaving Mr. Mackenzie,* the heroine, Julia Martin, is recovering from an experience of sexual betrayal and attempting a futile liaison with the decent but inadequate Mr. Horsfield. Julia is a recognizable Rhys heroine: a broken woman of uncertain age, the victim of an oversensitive nature, of emotional abuse, and of other quotidian cruelties of ordinary life. Sadly, Julia finds relief only in brief outbursts of rage. In some ways Julia is Rhys's most self-centered protagonist: though acutely sensitive to her own woes, she is only rarely aware of the reality of others'. Rhys clearly implies that her heroine is at least partly responsible for the mess she finds herself in.

Resources

A great deal of information about Jean Rhys is available, in addition to the bibliographic material cited above.

Books and Writers. This is a very useful Web site for biographical background, as well as for links to Creole literature and other areas of inquiry (http://www.kirjasto.sci.fi/rhys.htm).

Imperial Archive. This Web site, dedicated to the study of literature, imperialism, and postcolonialism, is a valuable on-line source of information about Caribbean literature, the branch of current literary scholarship that is most actively engaged in the examination of Rhys's writings (http://www.qub.ac.uk/en/imperial/imperial.htm).

Jean Rhys Page. A useful starting point for on-line research on Rhys, this site links to many academic and course sites that contain helpful information about Rhys and her works (http://www.angelfire.com/hi/JeanRhys/).

Jean Rhys Papers. In 1976 the McFarlin Library at the University of Tulsa established this archive with the acquisition of the correspondence between Rhys and Selma Vaz Dias. Other collections were added and today the inventory of the archive is available on-line (http://www.lib.utulsa.edu/Speccoll/rhysj0I.htm).

Sidney F. Huttner, the library's curator of special collections, also administers a listserv (essentially, a private electronic message board) for scholars of Rhys.

BRIAN BLACK

Mordecai Richler

BORN: January 27, 1931, Montreal, Canada
DIED: July 3, 2001, Montreal, Canada
IDENTIFICATION: Canadian novelist, essayist, humorist, and satirist and one of his nation's most controversial and prolific journalists.

SIGNIFICANCE: Mordecai Richler, who resided variously in Paris, Spain, and England before returning to live in his native Montreal, wrote, more than 300 journalistic articles that appeared in a wide range of Canadian, U.S., and British publications. Rarely has a writer been so defined by the experiences of his life and personality. In his novels, which were often set within the Canadian Jewish community, Richler typically combined fantastic and wildly comic elements with a realistic theme. His many awards include two Canadian Governor General's Awards (1968, 1971), a Screenwriters Guild of America Award (1974), and a Ruth Schwartz Children's Book Award (1976).

A third-generation Canadian Jew, Mordecai Richler was born on January 27, 1931, in Montreal, where his grandfather settled after venturing to Canada in 1904 to escape persecution in eastern Europe.

Childhood. Richler grew up in a self-contained world circumscribed by Jewish orthodoxy and by fear and ignorance of French and English Canadians. He attended a local Jewish school, studied the Talmud, and was expected to become a rabbi. At Baron Byng High School (the Fletcher's Field of his fiction), a Protestant school, he began to ease away from orthodoxy and to conceive of himself as both Jewish and Canadian, though this complementary conception was not always easy.

Education. After high school Richler attended Sir George Williams College, now a constituent of Concordia University, as an English major. He found several first-year courses uninspiring and, in fact, satirized them in his early work. It was here, however, that he developed a strong interest in contemporary literature and journalism. Once he was sure he wanted to write, he abandoned college after two years and left Canada for Europe, which had attracted him since boyhood. Richler would later say that he had made this decision because he was afraid of being enmeshed and devitalized by academic life and also because Europe offered the promise of excitement and adventure. Richler felt that Canada was "culturally barren" and that he needed the challenge of Europe to become a world-class writer.

The Aspiring Author. At 19 Richler moved to Europe and wrote *The Acrobats* while living mainly in a run-down hotel room in Paris. Alone at first, he later became part of a circle of aspiring North American writers that included Allen Ginsberg, Terry Southern, and Mavis Gallant, all of whom had made similar literary pilgrimages to Paris.

This photograph, taken in 1960, shows a float burning during the Valencia festival of *Les Falles.* This festival, which Richler attended in 1952 and wrote about in *The Acrobats,* is held every year in honor of Valencia's patron saint, San José. Elaborate floats are constructed as well as huge papier-mâché dolls called *ninots.* These floats and dolls are then set alight in the streets on the *Nit de Foc,* or night of the fire.

It was here that Richler began writing seriously and had his first significant piece published. A slight short story, "Shades of Darkness: Three Impressions," appeared in *Points,* a Parisian magazine for young writers. As the subtitle indicates, this story of three misfits involves three separate impressions. The work is an early illustration of Richler's credo—the writer has the moral responsibility to be the "loser's advocate."

Richler made several trips outside Paris, to Normandy, Cambridge (where he visited the British writer E. M. Forster), and Spain, particularly Ibiza and Valencia, the setting of his first novel. He remained in Spain, "rooted" there for almost a year. While in Valencia during 1952, he participated in his first *fallas,* the Spanish ritualistic bonfire, which features prominently in *The Acrobats.* He perceived his participation as a rite of passage, a final, irrevocable commitment to writing: ". . . those flames in Valencia consumed . . . a host of personal devils. . . .

FILMS BASED ON RICHLER'S WORK

1974 *The Apprenticeship of Duddy Kravitz*

1977 *Jacob Two-Two Meets the Hooded Fang*

1979 *The Wordsmith*

1985 *Joshua Then and Now*

1999 *Jacob Two-Two Meets the Hooded Fang*

Florence Wood Richler, the author's second wife, enjoys a humorous moment while he looks on with a deadpan expression.

Gone with the flames went the guilt acquired by leaving college without a degree . . . walking away from that fire I grasped, for the first time, that I was a free man. I owed no apologies. My life was mine to spend as I pleased." In 1954 he married a Canadian, Catherine Boudreau, and they moved to London, where he spent the next 10 years writing television and movie scripts, including treatments for *Room at the Top* and its sequel, *Life at the Top.*

The First Novel. Richler completed *The Acrobats* in Paris and submitted it to a literary agent on his way back to Canada. He soon learned that André Deutsch was willing to publish it with revisions. He revised the novel three times on the suggestion of his editors and agent. After the third revision Richler said to them, "I am no longer truly involved with *The Acrobats* and am wary of doing too much tampering. . . . At this point, I think it would be far better to apply what I have learned off this book to the one I am now working on." During this period Richler worked as a radio editor for the Canadian Broadcasting Company (CBC) in Montreal. Deutsch had offered him an advance of 100 pounds ($250). "I don't get you," Richler's Uncle Jake said to him, "You put two years into writing a book and now you're happy because some jerk in London has offered you a lousy two-fifty for it. You could have earned more than that cutting my lawn."

Richler was dispatched by André Deutsch to Toronto to impress the Canadian distributor, who instead pointed out the grim truth: "No serious Canadian novelist—including Morley Callaghan or Hugh MacLennan—is able to support himself strictly on the sale of his novels in Canada." The distributor was prepared to risk a first order of 400 copies for all of Canada. As Richler reported, "I stood to earn approximately $32, if they sold out." Yet Richler's career blossomed, particularly because of the gritty reality his writing conveyed.

Remarriage and the Return Home. Soon after moving to London, he met Florence Wood, then an actress and fashion model and married to the Canadian screenwriter Stanley Mann. They divorced their respective mates and married in 1960. Florence had one child from her union with Mann and together she and Richler had four more. The Richlers returned to Montreal in 1972 and, until Mordecai's death, maintained a residence in Quebec, spending most of their time in a house on Lake Memphramagog. Despite his ongoing battles over politics, Richler always harbored a fondness for Quebec.

Richler once said he returned home after 20 years in England because, after *St. Urbain's Horseman,* he felt he could not write any more novels there. "I hadn't been brought up there. If I stayed there, I would have had to become a film writer, not a novelist. I had to come back to my roots and a society I understood better."

A Writer for the World. Richler wrote *Cocksure* at the close of a 20-year sojourn in London. He moved back to Montreal to find himself in the midst of an alleged "Canadian renaissance," a cultural flowering of a young nation eager to cast off both colonial ties to the mother country and cultural oppression from the south. While Richler was out of the country, Canada had acquired the Governor General's Award for literature and Canada Council grants for writers, as well as an elaborate public subsidy program for Canadian publishing houses, which ensured an active publishing market.

While such changes in Canada made Richler's success simpler, he had already begun writing for a larger, non-Canadian audience. In addition to his novels, Richler continued to be a scriptwriter and a journalist. While he dismissed scriptwriting as a means of buying time for his novels and as a form not worthy of the serious novelist, journalism was another matter. His work has appeared since the 1950s in publications such as *Punch, New Statesman, Commentary, Kenyon Review, The Atlantic Monthly, The New York Times Book Review, Saturday Night, Canadian Literature, Playboy, Life,* and *Weekend Magazine.* No matter what form he wrote in, Richler celebrated traditional virtues and the importance for his characters and readers to search for and discover their validity.

Mordecai Richler wrote in a variety of styles and forms. During his long career, Richler won the Governor General's Award for literature in 1968 for *Cocksure* and again in 1971 for *St. Urbain's Horseman*. He was also awarded the Commonwealth Writers Prize in 1990 for *Solomon Gursky Was Here*. He also published collections of essays, an autobiography, *The Street* (1972), and a memoir, *This Year in Jerusalem* (1974).

Ethnicity and Poverty. Richler was said to be intense and politically incorrect or even irreverent; according to one critic, Richler's career had three major phases of focus—first, he offended Jews; then English Canadian nationalists; and finally Quebec separatists. Richler remembered every detail of his working-class childhood in Montreal and the rare glimpses he got of the would-be gentrified Jews in the suburbs of Outremont and Westmount, and some of those details were too funny to let go. In *Solomon Gursky Was Here*, it all comes together at the 75th birthday gala of Bernard Gursky in a satirical dissection of the charity banquet circuit. Richler writes, "They took turns declaring each other governors of universities in Haifa or Jerusalem or Man of the Year for State of Israel Bonds. Their worthiness [was] certified by hiring an after-dinner speaker to flatter them for a ten-thousand-dollar fee, the speaker coming out of New York, New York—either a former secretary of state, a TV star whose series hadn't been renewed, or a Senator in need."

Humor of Everyday Life. Richler's considerable talent for the comic is displayed in *The Incomparable Atuk*

(1963), a zany novel discussing Canadian nationalism, and in *Cocksure,* a comical-satirical account of the difficulty of adhering to traditional values in a world gone mad. *St. Urbain's Horseman* and *Joshua Then and Now* (1980) use this same humorous tone to go beyond the settings, characters, and concerns of the preceding novels. *St. Urbain's Horseman* ex-

This photograph by Thierry Cariou, entitled *People Walking,* evokes in the viewer a feeling of uncertainty that mirrors the ambiguity and paradoxes not only of Richler's characters but of his works as well.

HIGHLIGHTS IN RICHLER'S LIFE

1931	Mordecai Richler is born in Toronto, Canada, on January 27.
1948	Attends Sir George Williams College.
1950	Moves to Paris.
1951–1952	Interacts with other aspiring writers and begins work on *The Acrobats*.
1952	Witnesses the *fallas* event in Valencia, Spain, which he features in *The Acrobats*.
1952	Initial publication of first novel, *The Acrobats*.
1954	Marries Catherine Boudreau; moves to England.
1960	Divorces Boudreau; marries Florence Wood.
1968	Receives Governor General's Award for *Cocksure*.
1971	Receives Governor General's Award for *St. Urbain's Horseman*.
1972	Returns to Montreal.
1974	Receives Screenwriters Guild of America Award.
1976	Receives Ruth Schwartz Children's Book Award.
1990	Receives Commonwealth Writers Prize for *Solomon Gursky Was Here*.
1992	Becomes involved in debate over Quebec independence.
2001	Dies in Montreal, Canada, on July 3.

amines the personal, professional, and ethnic experiences of a 37-year-old man subjected to intense contradictory feelings, who, Richler has stated, is "closer to me than anybody else." *Joshua Then and Now* employs a complex pattern of flashbacks to explore the possessive nature of the past, the ironical inversions caused by the passage of time, and the sad aspect of mutability. *Jacob Two-Two Meets the Hooded Fang* (1975) and *Jacob Two-Two and the Dinosaur* (1987), two characteristic, hilarious children's novels, tell of the difficulties experienced by the young child in an adult world.

Journalism and Scriptwriting. Richler published over 300 journalism pieces in a wide range of publications. He published selections in *Hunting Tigers under Glass* (1968), *The Street* (1969), *Shovelling Trouble* (1972), *Notes on an Endangered Species* (1974), and *Home Sweet Home: My Canadian Album* (1984). His periodic ventures into scriptwriting, which he approached with less fervor than his journalism, have produced such scripts as *Life at the Top* (1965), *The Apprenticeship of Duddy Kravitz* (1974), *Fun with Dick and Jane* (1977), and *Joshua Then and Now* (1985).

Controversy and Politics. During spells between novels, Richler busied himself with numerous—and often highly irreverent and provocative—magazine and newspaper pieces, using satire to ridicule political and social targets.

The role of the antifascist International Brigades in the Spanish Civil War affected Richler's artistic works, especially his fiction. He honors the heroism of these brave bands of foreign volunteers in many of his works, including *The Acrobats, A Choice of Enemies, Joshua Then and Now, Son of a Smaller Hero,* and *St. Urbain's Horseman.* This Spanish Civil War poster for an International Brigade depicts the fever and fervor of the volunteers.

SOME INSPIRATIONS BEHIND RICHLER'S WORK

Two clusters of experience from Mordecai Richler's boyhood, one actual, the other vicarious, have had a marked effect on his artistic psyche: growing up in the Jewish community of Montreal during the 1930s and 1940s, of which he stated, "that was my time, my place, and I have elected myself to get it right," and his consciousness of the conflicts in Europe, particularly of the defense of Madrid, which made a strong impression on him as a boy of nine and later came to be used in his fiction as a metaphor for honor and heroism. The importance of these concurrent sets of experiences is pointed up by their repeated appearance in Richler's fiction and nonfiction. He focuses on both with equal intensity in *The Acrobats* and *Son of a Smaller Hero*, both of which may be considered first novels, defined by George Woodcock as works that present "somewhat realistically the problems, aspirations, and agonies of a young writer."

When the main character in *Duddy Kravitz* proved to be offensive to many Jewish readers, Richler remained fairly irreverent. He understood the concerns of the Jewish community, particularly when Jews argued that the character would provide ammunition to anti-Semites. Richler insisted that Duddy was never meant to be a metaphor for the Jewish people and was simply the type of kid with whom he had grown up. Richler wrote about his estrangements from both his mother, Leah, who hated his unflattering portrayal of a Jewish mother in *St. Urbain's Horseman*, and his orthodox father, Moses, with whom he had a fistfight when he was 13. They did not speak for two years. Brought up in the depression, Richler's childhood was a harsh struggle, but it provided colorful fodder for his early writings.

Two strong inspirations behind Richler's work were the exploits of the International Brigades and the writings of Ernest Hemingway. Here, news reporters mingle with members of an International Brigade during the Spanish Civil War. The man in the right center, with mustache and glasses, is Ernest Hemingway.

NONFICTION

1968 Hunting Tigers under Glass: Essays and Reports
1970 Canadian Writing Today
1972 The Street: A Memoir
1972 Shovelling Trouble
1974 Notes on an Endangered Species and Others (some of these essays also appear in Shovelling Trouble)
1977 Images of Spain (photographs by Peter Christopher with text by Richler)
1983 The Best of Modern Humour
1984 Home Sweet Home
1992 Oh Canada! Oh Quebec! Requiem for a Divided Country
1996 A Year in Jerusalem

FICTION

1954 The Acrobats
1955 Son of a Smaller Hero
1957 A Choice of Enemies
1959 The Apprenticeship of Duddy Kravitz
1963 The Incomparable Atuk
1968 Cocksure
1971 St. Urbain's Horseman
1980 Joshua Then and Now
1989 Solomon Gursky Was Here
1997 Barney's Version

CHILDREN'S FICTION

1975 Jacob Two-Two Meets the Hooded Fang

SCREENPLAYS

1965 Life at the Top
1974 The Apprenticeship of Duddy Kravitz
1977 Fun with Dick and Jane
1985 Joshua Then and Now

In turn, he was a target for cultural nationalists because he was forever taking potshots at Canadian pretensions and sensibilities.

Richler spoke out often on subjects ranging from sports to politics to publishing, but he always saved his most acidic words for his much-publicized (and often vilified) views on Quebec politics. Richler also fought a bitter and often lonely fight against Quebec separatism. Repeatedly, he sought to remind the separatists that, while Canada would be greatly diminished if Quebec left, so would the province itself. Almost from the beginning of his career, Richler, who was born on Montreal's St. Urbain Street, made a fairly regular habit of irking someone with his writing. For instance, the depiction of Montreal's Jewish community in his most famous novel, *The Apprenticeship of Duddy Kravitz,* offended many readers from that sector.

The Novelist. While *The Apprenticeship of Duddy Kravitz* (1959) offended some readers, it securely established Richler as an accomplished novelist. This scintillating portrait of a young Jewish entrepreneur in Montreal is characterized by an energizing authorial ambivalence and a contrast between the comic and the pathetic, by rich dramatic scenes, by a lively narrative pace, and by a comprehensive depiction of the protagonist as Montrealer, Jew, and individual. Richler's earlier novels, *The Acrobats* (1954), *Son of a Smaller Hero* (1955), and *A Choice of Enemies* (1957), which portray young, intense protagonists absorbed with finding proper values in a corrupt world, are essentially his own apprenticeship pieces.

BIBLIOGRAPHY

Abella, Irving, and Harold Troper. *None Is Too Many: Canada and the Jews in Europe, 1933–1948.* Toronto: Lester and Orpen Dennys, 1982.

Darling, Michael E., ed. *Perspectives on Mordecai Richler.* Toronto: ECW Press, 1986.

Davidson, Arnold E. *Mordecai Richler.* New York: F. Ungar, 1983.

Langer, Lawrence L. *The Holocaust and the Literary Imagination.* New Haven: Yale University Press, 1975.

McNaught, Kenneth. "Mordecai Richler Was Here." *Journal of Canadian Studies / Revue-d'Études-Canadiennes* 26, no. 4 (Winter 1992): 141–143.

Powe, B. W. *A Climate Charged.* Oakville, ON: Mosaic Press, 1984.

Ramraj, Victor J. *Mordecai Richler.* Boston: Twayne, 1983.

Sheps, G. David, *Mordecai Richler.* Toronto: Ryerson Press, 1971.

Strauss, Leo. *Liberalism Ancient and Modern.* New York: Basic Books, 1968.

Woodcock, George. *Mordecai Richler.* Toronto: McClelland and Stewart, 1970.

Richler and the Holocaust

Mordecai Richler neither had personal experience of the Holocaust nor did he specifically write about it. However, many critics agree that the event significantly impacted Richler's writing. North American Jewish writers have a different perspective from that of Elie Wiesel and other writers who actually lived through the experience of the Holocaust. "Yet," writes Rachel Feldhay Brenner, "the event of the Holocaust touches directly upon [the North American Jewish writer's] reality and undermines the psychological, historical and ideological framework of his existence." While the Holocaust occurred outside of Richler's experience, he and other Jewish writers found that they were obliged to come to grips with this event that, in an indirect fashion, had struck a profoundly significant blow at the reality of their world.

In Richler's work Montreal is the meeting place of the two cultures. His experience of growing up in Montreal in the 1930s in a predominantly Jewish neighborhood surrounded by a predominantly gentile world had exposed him to the complexity of the relationships between Jews and gentiles. The formative experience of his childhood became the cornerstone of Richler's writing, and he appointed himself to be its chronicler and interpreter. Ultimately, Richler believed that Jews and their French Canadian neighbors were equally responsible for the racial discord.

In his writing, Richler's response to the Holocaust alternates between two contrasting positions that emerge in much of post-Holocaust Jewish writing. Richler's urge to identify with Jewish suffering caused him to redefine and reassert his bonds with Judaism. At the same time, his strong ideological affinity with liberal humanism manifested itself in the desire to sever emotional bonds with the Jewish history of suffering and to integrate into the gentile world. In Richler's work, the event of the Holocaust constitutes a focal point of reference in his attempt to resolve his conflict of Jewish identity.

Richler's attitude is rooted in the history of anti-Semitism in Canada in the 1930s and 1940s. The Quebec of his childhood was influenced by the fascist movement led by Adrien Arcand. While this discrimination directed Richler's later attitude, he grew even more dissociated from Jewish tradition as he observed what he called "Jewish passivity" in the confrontation with a hostile world. In the background of Richler's writing is a constant tension between the acceptance of the Jewish history of persecution and the rejection of the assumption that the tradition of suffering must continue. The Holocaust, then, represented to Richler the strength of the Jewish identity but also its vulnerability.

At times liberal humanism offered a solution for Richler. For him as for other writers, this perspective grew directly from the experience of the Spanish Civil War, which is discussed in many of Richler's works. The war mobilized left-wing intellectuals, gentiles, and Jews to fight for the ideals of equality and freedom against the threat of fascism. The

Located in Thuringia, Germany, Fritz Cremer's sculpture *Revolt of the Prisoners,* ca. 1950, captures the vulnerability of the Jews and the horror of the Holocaust, but it also captures their courage and the rejection of passivity by the Jews who rose against their captors in an action they had to know would fail.

war, it seems, marked the end of the era in which one could clearly distinguish between the progressive political elements and the reactionary forces. Liberals, socialists, and communists saw the Spanish Civil War as the archetypal struggle between freedom and oppression. While many writers failed to maintain such a belief in the war effort afterward (not least because of the distasteful actions and embarrassing alliances of the Loyalists), Richler remained idealistic.

Critics have noted different stages in Richler's use of Jewishness in his work. Often such a serious perspective is couched in ironic humor. When he wrote nonfiction, though, Richler often openly condemned Jews for not maintaining a liberal perspective and joining humanistic efforts throughout the world. Richler tended to criticize Jews for what he perceived as their paranoid fear and mistrust of the gentiles. Ironically, his arguments are quite often punctuated by his own painful memories. Richler could not help recalling his own experience of anti-Semitic indignities, and owing to this recollection, he sometimes could not control his tremendous—at times well-nigh ungovernable—rage at the horror of the Holocaust.

SOURCES FOR FURTHER STUDY

Langer, Lawrence L. *The Holocaust and the Literary Imagination.* New Haven: Yale University Press, 1975.

Reader's Guide to Major Works

THE ACROBATS

Published: 1954
Genre: Social realism
Time period: Twentieth century
Setting: Spain, among a group of disillusioned expatriates

Themes and Issues. *The Acrobats* examines many themes that recur in Richler's later novels, among them the conflicts between races, generations, and traditions; the search for proper values; and the paradox of liberation as both creative and destructive. Certain elements of form and tone that were to become characteristic of Richler first appear here: the ambivalent protagonist through whose consciousness the novel is presented, ambiguous endings, set pieces of satire, suspenseful plotting, brilliant dramatic scenes, striking evocation of mood and setting, grotesque presentation of villains, and sympathetic portrayal of losers.

The Plot. The novel's protagonist, André Bennet, an Anglo-French Canadian, is a bewildered youth looking for absolutes in a world where it is difficult to distinguish right from wrong. He has come to Valencia, Spain, once the capital of the Loyalist government and now a squalid town, because of his admiration for the heroic International Brigades, who, because of their dedication to their cause, epitomize for him honor and truth, virtues he finds lacking in his own age. André's quest is conducted among characters that essentially serve as mouthpieces for various ideologies. At the end of the novel, André dies violently without realizing his quest, but the novel holds out the promise of a better world through the symbolic birth of a child named after him.

Analysis. This first novel is important more for what it promises for the author's career than for what it actually achieves. There is undeniably some appeal in its frank, intense, youthful perceptions, its evocation of mood, its portrayal of a few distinct characters, and its energetic use of language, but it is a flawed novel. As Richler realized even as he sent off his revised manu-

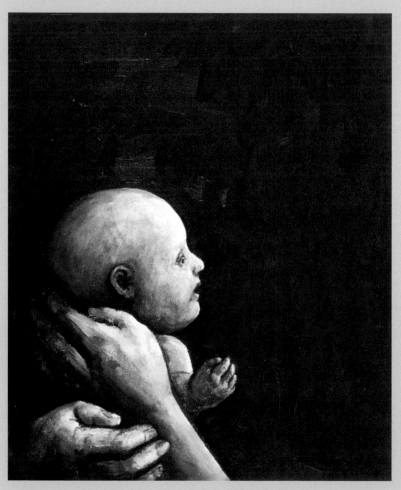

Artist Evelyn Williams depicts a baby looking forward, out toward an open, empty space in her 1994 oil-on-canvas painting *New Baby*. The promise of this new life perhaps mirrors the sense of promise that a baby's birth evokes at the end of Richler's novel *The Acrobats*.

script to the publisher, further revisions might have eliminated two main shortcomings: the subservience of character development to that of theme and the undigested influence of writers such as John Dos Passos, André Malraux, and Ernest Hemingway.

SOURCES FOR FURTHER STUDY

Craniford, Ada. *Fiction and Fact in Mordecai Richler's Novels*. Lewiston: Edwin Mellen Press, 1992.

THE APPRENTICESHIP OF DUDDY KRAVITZ

Genre: Novel
Subgenre: Social realism; satire
Published: 1959
Time period: 1950s
Setting: Montreal, Canada

Themes and Issues. Richler stated that he both admired and despised Duddy, a Jewish youth from the Montreal slums who claws his way to the top. This ambivalence about his character is patently evident in *The Apprenticeship of Duddy*

Kravitz and imparts to it a vitalizing tension and enriching complexity.

The Plot. A scintillating portrait of a young Montreal Jewish entrepreneur, the novel offers a contrast between the comic and the pathetic, as well as rich dramatic scenes, a lively narrative pace, and a comprehensive depiction of the protagonist as an individual. In the course of his obsessive quest for land and wealth ("a man without land is nobody," says his grandfather), Duddy repeatedly hurts the two people, Yvette and Virgil, who are trying the hardest to help him.

It is not surprising that this novel, which critics consider the best of Richler's early work and one of his finest novels, should have as its setting the Montreal of the 1950s. This is the world that haunts Richler's psyche. The assurance and confidence in this novel mark a new stage in the writer's development. The narrative pace is livelier than previously, and dramatic scenes are exceptionally well done. Humor is organic and integrated and is not simply relegated to set passages.

Actor Richard Dreyfuss is seen here starring in the title role of the 1974 film adaptation of Richler's novel *The Apprenticeship of Duddy Kravitz.* With the support of the reader or not, Duddy quests after wealth—and achieves it.

Analysis. Some critics have criticized Richler's portrayal of Duddy as being too quaint; others believe that it is too detached and too critical. Most likely, Richler's brilliant portrait of Duddy is neither. Richler is aware of both the good and the bad in his protagonist and is neither Duddy's castigator nor his advocate. He invites the reader to look objectively at Duddy, though the reader, like the author, may not be able to affirm full feelings for Duddy. In *The Apprenticeship of Duddy Kravitz,* Richler allows the theme to emerge organically from the natural evolution of narrative and protagonist.

SOURCES FOR FURTHER STUDY

Cluett, Robert, and Suzanne Ives. "An Art of Objects: The Language of *The Apprenticeship of Duddy Kravitz.*" In *Perspectives on Mordecai Richler,* edited by Michael E. Darling. Toronto: ECW Press, 1986.

THE INCOMPARABLE ATUK

Genre: Novel
Subgenre: Social realism; satire
Published: 1963
Time period: 1950s
Setting: Toronto, Canada

Themes and Issues. *The Incomparable Atuk* (*Stick Your Neck Out* was the title of the American edition) is a humorous investigation of Canadian life in the 1950s.

The Plot. In this novel Richler utterly disregards the element of probability in formulating

An Eskimo halts his canoe to look at pure white icebergs that float soundlessly by on a dark sea under a darkening sky in Rockwell Kent's haunting 1933 painting *Eskimo* (Pushkin Museum, Moscow). By contrast, Richler's Eskimo poet, Atuk, lives in the city of Toronto, a place alien to his heritage, and is revealed in the end as a pretentious and corrupt poet.

the central idea of the novel, which tells of the picaresque adventures of Atuk, an Eskimo poet, in Toronto. Initially Atuk appears to be an artless individual whose innocence is used to point out the foibles of the Toronto locals, but soon he is revealed to be equally corrupt and pretentious.

Analysis. Richler, who was still living in London at the time he wrote this novel, uses his farcical style to illuminate the lives and beliefs of North American writers exiled in Europe. According to Richler, when such intellects wrote about North America, they settled "on a style that did not betray knowledge gaps of day-to-day experience." On its publication, reviewers were not sure what to make of Richler's tone, and it is a question that continues to divide critics. Some thought the book a black comedy, while others saw only light satire and lack of substance. Still others took no firm stand on Richler's intent. Some critics argued that *The Incomparable Atuk* was flawed because it focused on dated and regional matters. While some Canadian reviewers responded to the novel as a roman à clef, one American dismissed it as an in-joke for "hip Canadians." However understood, *The Incomparable Atuk* is a lot of fun.

SOURCES FOR FURTHER STUDY
Craniford, Ada. *Fiction and Fact in Mordecai Richler's Novels.* Lewiston: E. Mellen Press, 1992.

COCKSURE
 Genre: Novel
 Subgenre: Satire
 Published: 1968
 Time period: 1960s
 Setting: London, England

Themes and Issues. *Cocksure* has the extravagant plotting and fantastic characterization of *The Incomparable Atuk,* but it is quite evidently neither as parochial nor as frivolous.

The Plot. Though *Cocksure* focuses on the misadventures of a Canadian innocent, Mortimer

Griffin, in swinging London of the 1960s, it is not primarily concerned with Canadian issues. While leaning heavily on grotesque elements and employing often very ribald language, the novel looks unsparingly at the ubiquitous decline of spiritual values and moral responsibility in contemporary society at large. Richler portrays Griffin as feckless, bumbling, and more naïve than innocent and pokes fun at him. Yet Richler is clearly on Griffin's side when he confronts his corrupt society.

Richler appears to be more angered than amused by the forces generating this decline in values and moral responsibility. Consequently, the humor is more militant, the imagery more grotesque, and the language more ribald than in *The Incomparable Atuk.* Written at a time when Richler was regularly involved with scriptwrit-

Richler's satirical novel *Cocksure* takes place in swinging London during the 1960s. Many placed the blame for the rapid decline of spiritual values and moral responsibility that seemed to begin at that time on the introduction of the miniskirt. The model Twiggy, so called because of her thin, angular build, which was unusual in the modeling world of that time, became the poster girl for the Swinging Sixties. In this photograph, taken in 1966, she is shown wearing a minidress.

ing, *Cocksure* invites analysis in cinematic terms. There are numerous scenes where Richler employs techniques that suggest montages, cuts, and dissolves, and the pervasive dialogue, which at times contributes incrementally to the narrative and at others explodes with appealing wit, could quite easily have been lifted from a film script.

Analysis. The grotesquerie and ribaldry, which some interpreted as obscenity, were responsible for the mild sensation the novel occasioned on publication: certain bookstores in Britain refused to stock it, and Ireland, Australia, New Zealand, and South Africa banned it altogether. Though it is Richler's most pervasively satirical novel, it never becomes a cogent, thoroughgoing satire. In fact, many of the early reviewers felt that Richler succeeded more in entertaining than in vexing the world.

The novel firmly established Richler as a writer of international stature. It was translated into several languages, including Dutch, Italian, and Japanese. An extract won the Paris Review Annual Prize for humor. In Canada, the novel won Richler the Governor General's Award.

SOURCES FOR FURTHER STUDY
Craniford, Ada. *Fiction and Fact in Mordecai Richler's Novels.* Lewiston: E. Mellen Press, 1992.

ST. URBAIN'S HORSEMAN
   Genre: Novel
   Subgenre: Social realism; satire
   Published: 1971
   Time period: 1960s
   Setting: London

Themes and Issues. *St. Urbain's Horseman* examines the personal, professional, and ethnic experiences of a 37-year-old man subjected to intense, contradictory feelings about his existence in the modern world.

The Plot. The protagonist, Jake Hersh, a Canadian currently living in London, is older than Richler's previous characters. Hersh has varied experiences relating to his roles as a family man, as an artist, and as an individual conscious of his ethnic and national roots. Moreover, his obsession with reviewing his life occasions major flashbacks to his boyhood, youth, and early manhood.

Richler draws heavily on his own experiences for this novel; he has observed that Jake is closer to him than any of his other protagonists. There are many parallels between their lives. Like Richler, Hersh spends his boyhood and adolescence in Montreal, admires the International Brigades, flees his stifling Jewish and Canadian environment for London where he intends to prove himself, makes trips to Israel and Germany, marries a gentile, has divorced parents, and returns in 1967 to Montreal for his father's funeral. A few accounts of Hersh's experiences in the novel are actually taken verbatim from published bits of Richler's memoirs with the first person changed to Hersh.

This oil-on-canvas painting, *A Knight on a Galloping Charger,* attributed to the circle of August Querfurt, an eighteenth-century German painter, evokes the elusive figure of the Horseman that Richler used as a multiple symbol in *St. Urbain's Horseman.*

Hersh's sensibility and beliefs also are similar to Richler's. Like his creator, he is apprehensive of aging, feels he belongs to a frivolous generation, is a socialist but distrusts professional liberals and the masses, is ambivalent toward Canada, strives to be a devoted family man, and celebrates "decency, tolerance, honor." Richler makes no conscious effort to hide the similarities, although *St. Urbain's Horseman* is a novel and not an autobiography. It has more incidents imaginatively conceived than drawn unchanged from Richler's own experience.

Analysis. In *St. Urbain's Horseman,* Richler introduces the most complex and challenging symbol of his writing: the Horseman. Critics have offered different interpretations of this elusive figure, perceiving him variously as Jake's conscience, as the "redeeming manhood for Jewish men," as the "redemptive deliverer" of the Jews, and as a "metaphor for the triumph of art." Each of these interpretations gives the Horseman a single, fixated meaning. However, Richler, who has stated that the novel "functions on several levels," evidently intends him as a symbol with multiple meanings, which vary in the three separate spheres of the novel: the domestic and social, the racial and ethnic, the professional and artistic.

In the first sphere, the Horseman is a false god, advocating dubious values. In the second, he is, when considered within the cyclical pattern of Hersh's dreams and nightmares, part of Richler's ambitious attempt to create a myth for the contemporary Jew who, having "not gone like sheep to the slaughterhouse" in Auschwitz and being "too fastidious to punish Arab villages with napalm," did not "fit a mythology." In the third sphere, the Horseman represents the artist's desire for participation, which is constantly in conflict with his inherent role as an observer.

This multiple symbolic function of the Horseman, together with the involved narrative, the skillful structural use of layers of flashbacks, the extensive gallery of memorable secondary characters (including a middle-aged Duddy Kravitz), and the penetrating portrait of a troubled, ambivalent protagonist, makes this novel a very dense work and has encouraged several critics to consider it Richler's best novel. It garnered the Governor General's Award in 1971.

SOURCES FOR FURTHER STUDY

Tausky, Thomas E. "St. Urbain's Horseman: The Novel as Witness." In *Perspectives on Mordecai Richler,* edited by Michael E. Darling. Toronto: ECW Press, 1986.

SOLOMON GURSKY WAS HERE

Genre: Novel
Subgenre: Magic realism; satire
Published: 1989
Time period: Late nineteenth and early twentieth centuries
Setting: Quebec and England

Themes and Issues. In what some critics call his best novel, *Solomon Gursky Was Here,* Richler used characters to make clear his strong feelings about Canada's ethnic composition. "Let me put it this way. Canada is not so much a country as a holding tank filled with the disgruntled progeny of defeated peoples. French-Canadians consumed by self pity; the descendants of Scots who fled the Duke of Cumberland; Irish, the famine; and Jews, the Black Hundreds. Then there are the peasants from Ukraine, Poland, Italy, and Greece, convenient to grow wheat and dig out the ore and swing the hammers and run the restaurants, but otherwise to be kept in their place. Most of us are huddled tight to the border, looking into the candy store window, scared of the Americans on one side and the bush on the other."

The Plot. A huge, multigenerational saga, *Solomon Gursky Was Here* follows Moses Berger in his quest to discover the mysterious particulars of the life of Solomon Gursky, scion of the powerful Gursky family. Berger's journey takes him across continents, from the Great White North to London, and through painful segments of his own life. Ravens, creators and tricksters, appear frequently in this garrulous, bighearted book; they hover over Solomon Gursky's life like a black-feathered question who have lived a convoluted, endearingly manic saga. The task of navigating this labyrinth falls to Moses Berger, the biographer of Ephraim's grandson Solomon (1899–1934). Moses is a writer and lover manqué, a former academic, a semirecovered alcoholic, and the novel's hero by default—his job is less that of a chronicler than of an explorer and private eye as he follows the angles that lead him deeper into the heart of Gursky darkness.

Analysis. In this, his ninth and most complex novel, the typical Richler scenes—funny, biting, snide, and sympathetic takes on Montreal Jewish life—are incorporated into a fanciful superstructure of history, geography, myth. For as it turns out, the Gurskys have participated in nearly every big moment of Canadian (and world) history, from the first Arctic explorations to Mao's Long March to Watergate and Entebbe.

Richler assembles a huge cast of characters and renders each in loving detail. The mythical elements of Berger's quest, however, and the fantastical speculations about Gursky's life are what raise this novel to the first rank. The prose allows Richler to both satirize with efficiency and transcend satire. *Solomon Gursky Was Here* features stories within stories and a bittersweet resolution. On its deepest level, though, with all its gleeful obscenity and dirty dealings, *Solomon Gursky Was Here* is a moral novel. Rage—moral rage—fuels Mordecai Richler's imagination, and it is most evident in this complex novel.

SOURCES FOR FURTHER STUDY

Todd, Richard. "Narrative Trickery and Performative Historiography: Fictional Representation of National Identity in Graham Swift, Peter Carey, and Mordecai Richler." In *Magical Realism: Theory, History, Community,* edited by Lois Parkinson Zamora and Wendy B. Faris. Durham, NC: Duke University Press, 1995.

An important figure in Inuit (Eskimo) history and legend is the raven. It is credited with doing many wonderful things, including bringing light to the world, often through trickery or by the use of magical powers. Richler uses the raven as a tool throughout his novel *Solomon Gursky Was Here.* Shown here is a detail of the 1999 *Sculpture de Nord (Sculpture of the North)* by Sonny MacDonald, John Sabourin, Eli Nasogaluak, and Armand Vaillancourt. Symbolic of its place in Inuit culture, the raven is of central importance in the sculpture.

mark, and ultimately, the myth of Gursky's life overwhelms Berger: whenever he approaches the truth, it flies farther away.

Details of the life of Ephraim Gursky (1817–1910) become a major part of the novel, including his experiences as a Jewish Eskimo shaman, a Minsk cantor in London (c. 1830), a pickpocket, a Newgate prisoner, a bogus millenarian preacher, and a Klondike roustabout. Popping up all over the globe and working dozens of shadowy scams, Ephraim represents only the first of the generations of Gurskys,

Other Works

SON OF A SMALLER HERO (1955). *Son of a Smaller Hero* describes the teeming streets, frustrated passions, and furious inbred lives of Montreal's Jewish quarter. It provoked a sharp reaction for its apparent put-down of some aspects of Jewish life and tradition. This work vividly re-creates the Montreal community of Richler's childhood and provides an incisive study of the growth of a sensitive, intense Jewish youth, Noah Adler, in this environment. Though the novel focuses on Jewish society and Jewish characters, Richler is not preoccupied with ethnic issues. As in all his fiction set in Jewish communities and peopled by Jews, he looks beneath the racial to the human and uses the Jewish world as a metaphor for human experience. The novel is at once Jewish, Canadian, and universal.

A CHOICE OF ENEMIES (1957). During his time in Britain, Richler supplemented his income writing television and film scripts. This experience inspired his novel *A Choice of Enemies,* about Canadian and American directors and writers forced by the McCarthy hearings to live in England. The protagonist of the novel, Norman Price, is a Canadian professor who has sacrificed his secure job at an American university for his Marxist beliefs and now makes a living as a scriptwriter and a popular novelist. Like André Bennet in *The Acrobats,* he yearns for what he considers the political integrity of men like his father, who gave up a lucrative Montreal medical practice to fight and die in Spain as a member of the International Brigades. Norman's involvement with Sally, a young Canadian, and Ernst, a refugee from East Germany, makes him realize that being victimized by bigotry is not exclusive to the left wing. Like the survivors of *The Acrobats,* he eventually comes to believe that what is important is not political commitments or alliances but adherence to "small virtues," to the traditional spiritual values of honesty, goodness, and honor in one's everyday relationships with one's fellow man.

JOSHUA THEN AND NOW (1980). *Joshua Then and Now* could be read as a companion piece or a sequel to *St. Urbain's Horseman.* The novel employs a complex pattern of flashbacks to explore the possessive nature of the past, the ironical inversions caused by the passage of time, and the sad aspect of mutability. The protagonist, Joshua Shapiro, is similar in temperament and sensibility to Jake Hersh. Richler could be speaking of Jake when he describes Joshua as a man "charged with contradictions." Though Joshua is not so intensely introspective as Jake, he too is neurotically insecure in

The Chilean artist Maria Illanes's twentieth-century painting *Desperation* captures the insecurity and torment of Richler's protagonist Joshua Shapiro in *Joshua Then and Now.*

his social and family life; he adheres to traditional moral values yet has a perceptible streak of malice in him; he is sympathetic yet sardonic; he has nightmares about his gentile wife's infidelity; he is tormented by fear of real and imagined Nazi butchers; and he is obsessively conscious of his mortality. Both Joshua and Jake were born in Montreal and lived in similar domestic and communal environments, though particulars differ. Both developed artistic interests—Jake as film director and Joshua as a journalist and occasional historian of the International Brigades. Both fled their constricting homeland for Paris, Spain, and London, and in both novels there are numerous flashbacks to the protagonists' childhood and youth in Montreal and their early manhood in Europe. The action of the earlier novel occurs in 1967, when Jake is in his late thirties; in *Joshua Then and Now,* it is 1977, and Joshua, ten years older than his predecessor, has returned to live in Montreal.

Resources

Although scholarship on Mordecai Richler appears to be in its infancy, readers who wish to learn more about him may be interested in the following:

Canadian Authors Association. Richler worked extensively to help promote writing in Canada. His efforts are continued by the Canadian Authors Association and other organizations. Canadian literary links are brokered through the Web site Northwest Passages: Canadian Literature Online (http://www.nwpassages.com/).

Documentary Film. Richler was the subject of a 1986 documentary, *The Apprenticeship of Mordecai Richler,* produced by the National Film Board of Canada. The film traces the sources of Richler's fiction through his own upbringing. It also contains clips from the film versions of many of his books. A clip of the film can be viewed on-line (http://cmm.nfb.ca/E/titleinfo/index.epl?id=16250&recherche=simple&coll=onf).

Mordecai Richler. This site, based at Harvard, contains a brief biography, a listing of titles, and a filmography. In addition, the site links to extensive information about a wide range of other Canadian authors (http://Schwinger.harvard.edu/~terning/bios/Richler.html).

University of Calgary. The major depository for Richler's papers is contained at the university library's special collections division. An inventory and biographical essay is accessible at the division's Web site (http://www.ucalgary.ca/library/SpecColl/richler.htm).

BRIAN BLACK

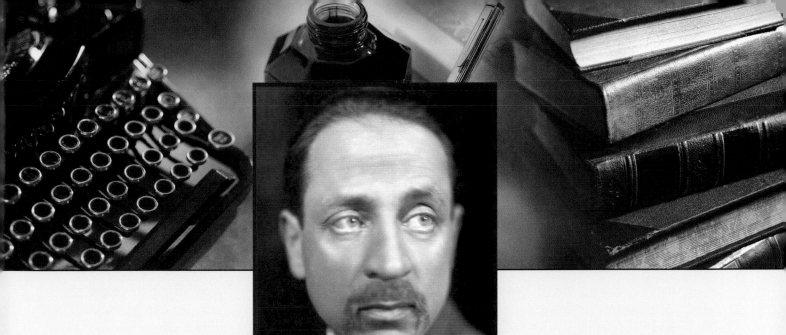

Rainer Maria Rilke

BORN: December 4, 1875, Prague, Bohemia (now the Czech Republic)
DIED: December 29, 1926, Valmont, Switzerland
IDENTIFICATION: Poet, playwright, and prose writer who, writing in German, was one of the most influential figures of literary modernism.

SIGNIFICANCE: Rainer Maria Rilke wrote some prose—notably *The Notebooks of Malte Laurids Brigge*—but is best known for his poetry, especially two masterworks, the *Duino Elegies* and the *Sonnets to Orpheus*. Frequently on the move, traveling extensively throughout Europe, Rilke was profoundly influenced by his visits to Russia, which he called his "spiritual fatherland." Most of his writing focuses on questions of religion, art, and love. His early work tends to be idea oriented and abstract, but the years he spent in Paris studying the sculptor Auguste Rodin turned him in a more descriptive, naturalistic direction. Nonetheless, the unseen world and the divine potential of the human soul remained his primary fascination.

The Writer's Life

Rainer Maria Rilke was born in Prague, Bohemia (part of Austria-Hungary), on December 4, 1875 (his actual first name was René; he changed it to Rainer in 1897). His childhood was unhappy, largely because of the unhappiness of his parents' marriage. His father was stiff and conventional, a former soldier turned railway official, while his mother was a flamboyant aspiring socialite. An infant sister had died before Rainer was born, and his mother treated him as if he were the daughter she had lost, dressing him in girls' clothes and calling him Sophia. "For my mother I was a plaything, I think, like a doll," he later wrote. She attempted to pass along to him her passionate Catholicism but was only partly successful; Rilke would remain alternately attracted to and repelled by formal religion for the rest of his life. His father tried to shape Rainer into a tough, rigid soldier like himself. After Rilke's parents separated when he was five, his father sent him to a military academy.

The young Rainer Maria Rilke at his desk in 1905. He believed in his work and came most fully to life during the isolated bursts when dozens of poems poured out from him. Sigmund Freud called him "one rather helpless in life" but also said he was "a great poet." The twentieth century agreed, and Rilke's body of work is considered a foundation stone of modernism. Rilke died at 51 after a lifetime of periodic low fevers and minor breakdowns. He moved from the home of one friend or patron to another, and said he didn't want to own a pet because of the emotional pain involved. At a reading in Vienna he suffered a nosebleed because holding so many conversations and looking people in the eye had caused his blood to pump too fast, but he soldiered through; the evening was a success.

Shy and inclined toward literature, Rilke was bullied by schoolmates and found the school's military atmosphere stifling. A sympathetic uncle intervened, and Rilke switched to a preparatory school in Linz, which was more suitable to his poetic sensibilities. By the time he enrolled at Carl-Ferdinand University in Prague in 1895 to study philosophy, literature, and art, he had already published his first book of poems, *Life and Songs*.

A Poet's Life. Rilke was miserable in highly structured, institutionalized settings, and although he was industriously devoted to his writing, women and travel were powerful at-tractions for him, too. In Linz, as a teenager, he had embarked on a romantic getaway to Vienna with a children's nurse. In 1897 in Munich, he had an affair with the Russian in-tellectual Louise ("Lou") Andreas-Salomé, an older woman who would remain an influential friend and supporter. He traveled to Italy, Sweden, Denmark, and perhaps most signifi-cantly, to Russia, where he met the novelist Leo Tolstoy, the poets Leonid and Boris Pasternak (father and son), and Leon Trotsky, the revolu-tionary. To the residue of his mother's orthodox religiosity, Rilke added a fascination with the Christian mysticism he encountered in Russia.

In 1900 Rilke joined an artists' colony at

The spires of Prague, capital of today's Czech Republic. Rilke grew up here when it was the second city of the Austro-Hungarian Empire, behind Vienna. In childhood Rilke had been intimidated by his hometown; returning as an adult he was somehow disappointed to find it cut down to size. "It makes me sad to see these houses at the corners, these windows and porticos, squares and church-roofs, to see them all humbled, smaller than they were, abased and completely in the wrong," he wrote in a letter.

Worpswede, Germany, where he met the sculptor Clara Westhoff. Rainer and Clara were married in March of the next year, and the following December their daughter, Ruth, was born. Clara was a student of the French sculptor Auguste Rodin, and spurred by this connection to the master, Rilke left Clara (they never divorced, but the marriage was effectively over by mutual consent) and began writing a study of Rodin, which was published in 1903. He would live in Paris for the next 12 years, serving as Rodin's secretary for part of that time. While in Paris he wrote several books, including *The Book of Hours, New Poems,* and *The Notebooks of Malte Laurids Brigge,* generally considered his most important work of prose.

"Maybe Ten Good Lines." Rilke has his character Brigge say, "Poems amount to so little when you write them too early in your life. You ought to wait and gather sense and sweetness for a whole lifetime, and a long one if possible, and then, at the very end, you might perhaps be able to write ten good lines." Indeed, from the time Rilke wrote those lines in 1910, he would struggle to write poems that met these excruciatingly high standards. In the meantime, relying on the financial support of friends and patrons, he continued his extensive travels, which included trips to Egypt and Spain, and spent part of 1911 and 1912 as the guest of Princess Marie von Thurn und Taxis Hohenlohe at Duino, her castle near Trieste. While there, he agonized over a poetical work on angels but with little success. He returned to Paris until the outbreak of World War I, when, at the age of 40, he was conscripted into the Austrian army. As a literary celebrity and a somewhat frail one at that, he was destined for a desk job but was still subjected to extensive training that beat him down physically; at the same time the general military atmosphere beat him down spiritually. He was virtually useless in the war records department, and influential friends won him a release after six months.

Rilke resumed his travels, lodging with wealthy patronesses, corresponding prodigiously with friends, supporters, and admirers, and writing some verse in French. He was in Munich in 1918, during Germany's so-called November Revolution. He was sympathetic to the leftist movement and grieved at the execution of its leaders. In 1921 he moved into a villa at Muzot, in the Rhône River valley in Switzerland,

Rilke at 20, as drawn by Emil Orlik. The Prague artist didn't flatter Rilke in this sketch, but he did help him secure early contacts for his literary career.

HIGHLIGHTS IN RILKE'S LIFE

1875   René Karl Wilhelm Johann Josef Maria Rilke is born in Prague on December 4, to Josef and Sophie Entz Rilke.

1894   *Life and Songs,* first book of poetry, is published.

1895–1896   Rilke attends Carl-Ferdinand University in Prague.

1897   Meets Lou Andreas-Salomé; changes name from René to Rainer.

1900   Joins Worpswede artists' colony; meets the sculptor Clara Westhoff.

1901   Marries Clara in March; their daughter, Ruth, is born December 12.

1902   Rilke moves to Paris to work on Rodin monograph; separates from Clara; *Book of Images* is published.

1903   *Auguste Rodin* is published.

1905   *The Book of Hours* is published.

1907   *New Poems* is published.

1910   Rilke finishes *The Notebooks of Malte Laurids Brigge.*

1915–1916   Does military service in the War Records Office; is discharged in July and returns to Munich.

1918   Is present in Munich for the November Revolution.

1921   Moves into Château de Muzot, his home base for the rest of his life.

1923   *Duino Elegies* and *Sonnets to Orpheus* are published; Rilke visits the sanatorium in Valmont.

1925   Spends time in Paris and at Valmont.

1926   Travels to Ragaz and Sierre; is in Valmont from November; dies on December 29.

1927   Is buried January 2 in Raron in Wallis Canton, Switzerland.

which would serve as his home base for the remainder of his life. He resumed work on the Duino project and, in a sudden whirlwind of inspiration lasting three weeks, not only finished that work but began and completed an extensive, elegant collection of sonnets as well. *Duino Elegies* and *Sonnets to Orpheus,* published in 1923, remain his most famous works, their popularity and influence increasing with the passing years.

Visiting the home of the novelist Leo Tolstoy in Russia, the writer stands with his lover Lou Andreas-Salomé and the poet Spiridon Drozhzhin in July 1900. "I believe that Russia will give me the words for those religious depths of my nature that have been striving to enter into my work since I was a child," he wrote in a letter.

Fairy-Tale Ending. Rilke's health began to decline. Suffering from leukemia, he shuttled back and forth between Muzot and various sanatoriums. At home, while gathering roses from his garden for a visitor, he pricked his hand on a thorn. The little wound did not heal, and an infection set in and complicated his leukemia. He fell into a rapid decline and died in Valmont, Switzerland, on December 29, 1926, at the age of 51.

The Writer's Work

Rainer Maria Rilke wrote poetry, fiction, drama, and creative essays, mostly in German, although he wrote original poems in French late in his life and also translated work by other authors. While committed to his own writing, he was powerfully drawn to and inspired by the visual arts. Art (or more generally aesthetics), religion, and romantic love are his primary themes.

Issues in Rilke's Writings. From an early age Rilke was passionate about God, art, and love. His romantic relationships with women (and his dependencies on them) inspired and informed much of his poetry, grounding his reports on the seen and unseen worlds in a very human sensuality. This same sort of drive was reflected in his attraction to the visual arts. His wife, Clara, and, more particularly, Auguste Rodin tapped into a vision of the human spirit and did so with tangible, earthly (even earthy) materials. Rilke strove to do the same with his poetry—that is, describe the inner and unseen life in part by describing the physical world in exacting, sculptural detail. He referred to these poems as *Dinggedichte,* "thing poems." Rilke never adopted his mother's passionate Catholicism; if anything, those early years of being taken to church and forced to kiss the wounds in Christ's statuary feet inoculated him against any future affiliation with institutional religion. Nonetheless, in his own curious way he remained passionately religious for the rest of his life. As with many other poets and artists, Rilke's art, after a fashion, could be said to be his religion. In his travels to Russia, which he called his "spir-

itual fatherland," he encountered Christian mysticism, and over the years he married to it elements of Islamic and Jewish mysticism, as well as traces of Eastern religious influence. These dynamics—sex, aesthetics, and religion—combine in various ways in all Rilke's work.

Rilke's Literary Legacy. Rilke's travels resulted in acquaintances, associations, friendships, and intimacies with scores of Europe's most prominent artists, writers, and intellectuals, who admired Rilke's work during his lifetime and championed it even more after his death. Herman Hesse and W. H. Auden, two of

Auguste Rodin's *Portrait of V. S. Eliseyeva,* done in 1906. Rilke was the French sculptor's secretary from September 1905 to May 1906. He admired Rodin for turning ideas into solid objects and ambitions into finished work: "This is the essential, that you should not stop at dreams, at intentions, at being in the mood, but that you should transpose everything into *things* with all your strength."

modernism's most influential writers in German and English, sang Rilke's praises. Since then, 50 years ago and more, his reputation has grown only stronger. Other writers routinely include him in lists of the most important writers of the twentieth century, where he is grouped with figures such as James Joyce, W. B. Yeats, and T. S. Eliot. While many modern-day writers may not care for one or another of those figures, Rilke himself has enjoyed continuous and close to unanimously high regard. Of course, Rilke may not have been thinking ahead to the late twentieth and early twenty-first centuries, but as luck would have it, he seems to have hit on many issues that concern modern readers while avoiding many of the bugaboos that irritate them. In a sense, perhaps more than any other modernist, his works prefigure the sensibilities of postmodernism.

Rilke's work has been a magnet for translators. (*Duino Elegies* alone has generated more

Auguste Rodin (1840–1917). From a letter about the sculptor by Rilke: "I can hardly wait for the Master to return, he is work and sustenance; when he is near, the day has many more hours and sleep is more refreshing." However, Rilke was getting impatient to pursue his own work. The rupture came in May 1906, when Rilke forgot to tell his employer about a letter that had arrived. Eight months later Rilke would still describe a river as "swelling like a Rodin contour."

The people, places, and ideas that combined to shape Rainer Maria Rilke are too numerous to analyze in detail, but prominent among them are his mother; the Catholic Church; the military academy; countless writers; Russia; Christian mysticism; Lou Andreas-Salomé; the Danish poet Jens Peter Jacobsen; Rilke's wife, Clara; Auguste Rodin, Paul Cézanne, and many other artists; painting and sculpture in general; numerous patronesses; the French symbolist poets; the city of Paris, on the one hand, and the natural world, on the other; and of course, sex, birth, and death.

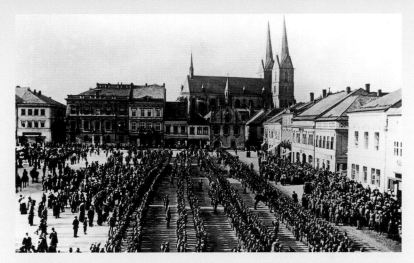

An Austro-Hungarian infantry musters for the front in 1914. Rilke was drafted at 40 and survived three weeks' barracks training before being sent to the Department of War Archives. His job there was to scan the dispatches and then write up anecdotes about frontline heroism, something he considered a "crooked and irresponsible misuse of literary activity"; at any rate, he couldn't produce anything usable. His commander was ready to treat the poet as a special case, but Rilke insisted on being of use during his service. A colleague wrote that at last the commander gave Rilke unlined paper to rule: "That was his contribution to the war. Industriously, he drew vertical and horizontal lines, for hours on end."

than 20 English translations), and he serves as the center of an ongoing lively debate on translation theory. Poets have argued that the non-poet translators have missed his vision and music in favor of a literal rendering of his words. Nonpoet translators have argued that the non-German-speaking poets have taken excessive liberties with Rilke's language in favor of their own poetic interpretations. Some have pointed to Rilke's own (English-to-German) translation of Elizabeth Barrett Browning's *Sonnets from the Portuguese* as a good model of how his own poetry should be translated.

BIBLIOGRAPHY

Baron, Frank, Ernest S. Dick, and Warren R. Maurer, eds. *Rilke: The Alchemy of Alienation*. Lawrence: Regents Press of Kansas, 1980.

Brodsky, Patricia Pollock. *Rainer Maria Rilke*. Boston: Twayne, 1988.

————. *Russia in the Works of Rainer Maria Rilke*. Detroit: Wayne State University Press, 1984.

Freedman, Ralph. *Life of a Poet: Rainer Maria Rilke*. New York: Farrar, Straus and Giroux, 1996.

Gass, William H. *Reading Rilke: Reflections on the Problems of Translation*. New York: Knopf, 1999.

Heep, Hartmut, ed. *Unreading Rilke: Unorthodox Approaches to a Cultural Myth*. New York: Peter Lang, 2000.

Kleinbard, David. *The Beginning of Terror: A Psychological Study of Rainer Maria Rilke's Life and Work*. New York: New York University Press, 1993.

Metzger, Erica A., and Michael M. Metzger. *A Companion to the Works of Rainer Maria Rilke*. Rochester, NY: Camden House, 2001.

Prater, Donald. *A Ringing Glass: The Life of Rainer Maria Rilke*. Oxford: Clarendon Press, 1986.

Ryan, Judith. *Rilke, Modernism and Poetic Tradition*. Cambridge: Cambridge University Press, 1999.

Schwarz, Egon. *Poetry and Politics in the Works of Rainer Maria Rilke*. New York: Ungar, 1981.

Reader's Guide to Major Works

THE BOOK OF HOURS
Genre: Poetry
Published: Leipzig, 1905

Themes and Issues. Rilke considered this, his tenth volume of poems, to be his first book of mature poetry. At the same time it provides a good contrast with his masterpieces of nearly 20 years later, *Duino Elegies* and *Sonnets to Orpheus*. The poetry here is more abstract, less rooted in concrete particulars of the physical world—and then only minimally and symbolically—and more concerned with the workings of the heart, mind, and soul. Rilke represses an instinct he is developing at the time, which he will pursue more wholeheartedly later, to express the unseen in the seen. For now, he asks, "Why am I reaching again for the brushes? / When I paint your portrait, God, / nothing happens. / . . . / But I can choose to feel you."

Analysis. Rilke's idea of this God he can choose to feel (an idea that implies that he can also choose not to) is vague enough to accommodate a range of theist and atheist interpretations. However, *The Book of Hours* resembles traditional mystical poetry, the word *mystical* being understood in its formal, religious sense rather than the casual, popular sense. In these poems Rilke expresses his struggle for union with God by means of introspective visions or journeys into the depths of his soul, or consciousness: "When gold is in the mountain / and we've ravaged the depths / till we've given up digging, / . . . / it will be brought forth into day." At least at this stage of Rilke's development, God—or what is divine in the individual—is the gold deep in the mountain of the self.

SOURCES FOR FURTHER STUDY

Clements, Arthur L. *Poetry of Contemplation*. Albany: State University of New York Press, 1990.

Freedman, Ralph. "*Das Stunden-Buch* and *Das Buch der Bilder*: Harbingers of Rilke's Maturity." In *A Companion to the Works of Rainer Maria Rilke*, edited by E. A. Metzger and M. M. Metzger. Rochester, NY: Camden House, 2001.

THE NOTEBOOKS OF MALTE LAURIDS BRIGGE
Genre: Novel
Subgenre: Fictionalized autobiography
Published: Leipzig, 1910
Time period: Early twentieth century
Setting: Paris, France

Themes and Issues. When Rilke finished writing *The Notebooks of Malte Laurids Brigge*, he wrote to his publisher, "Now everything can begin. . . . [A]fter [Malte] all songs are possible." He never wrote another novel, but *Malte* was a significant step beyond *The Book of Hours* toward *Duino Elegies* and *Sonnets to Orpheus*. In many respects this is an autobiographical work: like Rilke, Brigge is a poet who leaves his homeland to live in Paris, which initially repulses him, as it did Rilke. Rilke and Brigge also share some aesthetic sensibilities. At issue here, symbolically, are crises of identity: what it means to be an outsider, an artist, and to be caught between outcasts and the culture that casts them out.

The Plot. *Notebooks* does not have a plot in the conventional sense. It is the diary of a Danish poet who records and interprets what he sees and experiences in Paris along with memories of his past and his family, and it includes references to literature, art, and history. Brigge is appalled at the poverty and disease of the city and repulsed by its outcasts, the poor, sick, and dying. This confrontation with "ugliness," however, begins working a change on him: "I am learning to see. I don't know why it is, but everything enters me more deeply and doesn't stop where it used to. I have an in-

POETRY

1894 Life and Songs (Leben und Lieder)

1896 Offerings to the Lares (Larenopfer)

1896 Crowned by Dreams (Traumgekrönt)

1898 Advent

1899 In Celebration of Myself (Mir zur Feier)

1902 Book of Images (Das Buch der Bilder)

1905 The Book of Hours (Das Stunden-Buch)

1906 The Lay of the Love and Death of the Cornet Christoph Rilke (Die Weise von Liebe und Tod des Cornets Christoph Rilke)

1907–1908 New Poems (Neue Gedichte) (2 vols.)

1909 Requiem

1913 First Poems (Die frühen Gedichte)

1913 Life of the Virgin Mary (Das Marien-Leben)

1923 Duino Elegies (Duineser Elegien)

1923 Sonnets to Orpheus (Sonette an Orpheus)

1926 Valaisan Quatrains (Les quatrains Valaisans) (written in French)

1927 The Roses (Les roses) (written in French)

1927 The Windows (Les fenêtres) (written in French)

PROSE

1898 Along Life's Course (Am Leben hin)

1899 Two Stories from Prague (Zwei Prager Geschichten)

1900 Stories of God (Geschichten vom lieben Gott)

1903 Worpswede

1903 Auguste Rodin

1910 The Notebooks of Malte Laurids Brigge (Die Aufzeichnungen des Malte Laurids Brigge)

DRAMA

1897 Early Frost (Im Frühfrorst)

1898 Not Present (Ohne Gegenwart)

1902 Everyday Life (Das tägliche Leben)

LETTERS

1928 Letters to Rodin

1929 Letters to a Young Poet (Briefe an einen jungen Dichter)

1930 Letters to a Young Woman (Briefe an eine junge Frau)

1934 Letters to His Editor, 1906–1926

1935 Letters from Muzot, 1924–1926

1950 Correspondence in Verse with Erika Mitterer

1951 Correspondence with Marie von Thurn und Taxis

1952 Correspondence with Lou Andreas-Salomé

1952 Letters on Cézanne

1964 Wartime Letters of Rainer Maria Rilke

1974 On Poetry and Art (Über Dichtung und Kunst)

1986 Rilke and Russia: Letters, Reminiscences, and Poems

1987 Rainer Maria Rilke/Stefan Zweig: Letters and Documents

TRANSLATIONS

1908 Sonnets from the Portuguese (Elizabeth Barrett Browning)

1911 The Centaur (Maurice de Guérin)

1912 Love of the Magdalen

1913 Marianna Alcoforado: Portuguese Letters

1918 The Twenty-four Sonnets of Louise Labé

1925 Poems (Paul Valéry)

1936 Poems of Michelangelo

DUINO ELEGIES

Rainer Maria Rilke

Translated by David Young

---

terior that I never knew of." He is increasingly drawn to the outcasts, until he, too, falls victim to an untreatable nervous disease. Brigge is—as Rilke will vaguely urge later, in *Duino Elegies*—dying to the petty, deluded life and becoming a different creature, attuned to *real* reality. Brigge's diary simply ends, without any clear resolution, and the reader is left to assume that his metamorphosis has progressed to another stage.

Analysis. As well as charting Rilke's evolving belief system, *Notebooks* contains some startling language and some remarkable statements about poetry, which remains Rilke's first love. As noted earlier, he has Brigge say that one should collect a lifetime's worth of sense and sweetness "and then, at the very end, you might perhaps be able to write ten good lines." In other words, poetry must be the product of slow and agonizing cultivation. It should never simply be cranked out.

SOURCES FOR FURTHER STUDY

Schoolfield, George C. "Die Aufzeichnungen des Malte Laurids Brigge." In *A Companion to the Works of Rainer Maria Rilke*, edited by E. A. Metzger and M. M. Metzger. Rochester, NY: Camden House, 2001.

Sokel, Walter H. "The Devolution of the Self in *The Notebooks of Malte Laurids Brigge*." In *Rilke: The Alchemy of Alienation*, edited by Frank Baron, Ernest S. Dick, and Warren R. Maurer. Lawrence: Regents Press of the University of Kansas, 1986.

Ziolkowski, Theodore. *Dimensions of the Modern Novel: German Texts and European Contexts*. Princeton, NJ: Princeton University Press, 1969.

DUINO ELEGIES

Genre: Poetry
Subgenre: Elegiac verse
Published: Leipzig, 1923

Themes and Issues. Initiated at Duino Castle in 1912 and completed a decade later, *Duino Elegies* was envisioned as a progression from the "fundamental presuppositions" Rilke expressed in *The Book of Hours*. "There exists neither this world nor the world to come," he wrote in a letter, "but rather the great Unity, in which those beings who surpass us, the angels, are at home." The angels here are not the benign angels of Christianity. On the contrary, "Every angel is terrifying." They are like "lions who move so splendidly / that their magnificence does not recognize weakness," therefore they have no concern for the petty prayers of life-bound mortals, as expressed in the famous sentence that opens *Elegies*: "Who, if I screamed, would hear me among the angelic / orders?" In the "Eighth Elegy," Rilke says, "Animals see the world before them / with their whole eyes. Only our eyes / are turned inward, like traps." The inward looking of *The Book of Hours* does not suffice in this quest to achieve "the great Unity," neither can conventional religion help, as churches are as "useless as a Sunday post office." Yet the secular, sensual life is not the answer either, with its "fresh distractions" and "illusions of freedom."

Analysis. *Duino Elegies* is one of the great books of poetry of the twentieth century and has inspired readers around the world, influencing some of the most prominent contemporary poets, including Galway Kinnell, John Ashbery, and Robert Bly. It is difficult not to be dazzled by its unexpected language, stunned by its profound ideas, or moved by its tragedies, and it is difficult to decide whether one of those tragedies is not the impending death of the poet himself, just three years after the book's publication. The lines "O, to be dead at last, and know the stars," and "More life than I can hold / springs up in my heart," seem especially poignant. To be dead (whether literally or figuratively, it is the same here) to the hollow, tinny charade that absorbs mortals and blinds them to reality—this is precisely Rilke's point in this book.

SOURCES FOR FURTHER STUDY

Hollender, Christoph. "The Poet Meets the Mother of Invention: The Allegory of the Tenth Duino Elegy." In *Unreading Rilke: Unorthodox Approaches to a Cultural Myth,* edited by Hartmut Heep. New York: Peter Lang, 2000.

Komar, Kathleen L. "Rethinking Rilke's *Duineser Elegien* at the End of the Millennium." In *A Companion to the Works of Rainer Maria Rilke,* edited by E. A. Metzger and M. M. Metzger. Rochester, NY: Camden House, 2001.

———. *Transcending Angels: Rainer Maria Rilke's Duino Elegies.* Lincoln: Nebraska University Press, 1987.

Paulin, Roger, and Peter Hutchinson, eds. *Rilke's Duino Elegies: Cambridge Readings.* London: Duckworth and Ariadne, 1996.

Rilke in 1926 at the Sanatorium Valmont in Switzerland. He died that year of leukemia. In his notebook he wrote, "Now comes the last that I can recognize, \ pain, utter pain, fierce in the body's texture." He refused to take any drugs that might cause him to pass out.

SONNETS TO ORPHEUS

Genre: Poetry
Subgenre: Sonnet
Published: Leipzig, 1923

Themes and Issues. While working on *Duino Elegies* in 1922, Rilke experienced one of the most remarkable surges of inspiration and creative energy in literary history: In a three-week period he not only completed *Elegies* but wrote 55 formal sonnets, 26 of them in the first four days of that span alone. He described the period as "an indescribable storm, a hurricane in my mind and my spirit." Orpheus, from Greek mythology, is a mortal whose music is so powerful it charms gods and mortals alike and is even capable of raising the dead. In Rilke's *Sonnets*, Orpheus's music (combined with his love) is the answer to the questions raised in *Elegies*. With music, leavened with love, mortals can achieve that "great Unity" of the angels' existence, which casts a divine light on the mundane. The taste of an apple "wakes; is sheer translucence, / has double meaning, sunny, earthy, ours!" Music not only enables humans to see the beauty and meaning to which they have been blind, it facilitates their expression of that meaning and beauty, as well: "Dance the orange!" Rilke exhorts. With music in the world, Rilke can ask, "Does Time, the destroyer, really exist?"

Analysis. *Duino Elegies* and *Sonnets to Orpheus* stand alone, each a masterpiece in its own right, but in tandem they express the fullness of Rilke's vision. In *Elegies* Rilke stresses belief in the true reality of existence and the tragedy of ignorance to that reality. *Elegies* cries out for salvation, some bridge from the petty realm of humanity to the exalted realm of the angel. *Sonnets* explicitly identifies that salvation: music (poetry, art, the general song of the heart). What is more, Rilke's sonnets function as that music themselves—they are beautiful songs worthy of Orpheus.

SOURCES FOR FURTHER STUDY

Casey, Timothy. *A Reader's Guide to Rilke's "Sonnets to Orpheus."* Galway: Arlen House, 2001.

Holthusen, Hans. *Rainer Marie Rilke: A Study of His Later Poetry.* Translated by J. P. Stern. New Haven, CT: Yale University Press, 1952.

Keele, Alan. "Poesis and the Great Tree of Being: A Holistic Reading of Rilke's *Sonette an Orpheus.*" In *A Companion to the Works of Rainer Maria Rilke,* edited by E. A. Metzger and M. M. Metzger. Rochester: Camden House, 2001.

Other Works

AUGUSTE RODIN (1903). *Auguste Rodin* is not so much a biography of the sculptor as an exploration of his art. In this short work of praise, Rilke shares details of Rodin's life and information about his studios and how he works, but the descriptions and impressions of the sculptor's great works are the heart of this study. Rilke was overwhelmed by the way Rodin could render—in earthy material, with shapes and contours and textures—the inner workings of the soul, as well as the influences of the unseen world on the soul. Another feature of sculpture that fascinated Rilke was its universality, its independence from spoken or written language: "The language of this art was the body." Translation of this language would never be necessary. The book is somewhat worshipful and arguably devoid of genuine criticism. Rilke presents Rodin as a solitary laborer-prophet and reveals something of the sculptor but in the process, perhaps, reveals more about the poet himself. Certainly the most significant thing about this book is the pivotal point it represents in Rilke's development.

LETTERS TO A YOUNG POET (1929). Rilke corresponded prodigiously not only with friends and patrons, but with admirers as well.

In 1902, at the age of 27, long before *Elegies* and *Sonnets*, before *Malte Laurids Brigge,* and even before *The Book of Hours,* already a highly regarded literary figure, he received a letter from Franz Xaver Kappus, a 19-year-old youth in military school. Having been trapped in military school himself as a boy, Rilke instantly identified and sympathized with this young poet. He offers no advice on how to remedy specific flaws in Kappus's verse but instead shares generous advice on what it means to be a poet, and he suggests various approaches to seeing and experiencing and creating. He recommends books and identifies his most indispensable books as the Bible and the works of the Danish poet Jens Peter Jacobsen. He even offers advice on how to love, describing love as the alliance of two great solitudes. It is possible that, as Rilke's frequent translator Stephen Mitchell suggests, the older poet was in a sense writing back in time to a younger self.

THE LAY OF THE LOVE AND DEATH OF THE CORNET CHRISTOPH RILKE (1906). *Christoph Rilke,* a prose poem, went through various incarnations, the original draft being written in 1899 as *From a Chronicle—the Cornet (1664),* and the first published version being titled *The Lay of the Love and Death of the Cornet Otto Rilke.* The idea for this work came from some old records in the possession of Rilke's uncle that concerned a certain Christoph Rilke, presumed to be an ancestor to the poet, a young officer from Saxony who was killed in a campaign fought by the Austrian army against the Turks in northern Hungary in 1664. The work exhibits a very romanticized view of war, one that Rilke left behind after his own experience of World War I. Unfortunately, the poem was used extensively throughout the war to bolster patriotic fervor, a fact that disturbed Rilke greatly, but he had no copyright control.

A nineteenth-century etching by A. Fesca shows Castle Duino, left, overlooking the Gulf of Trieste. Rilke began *The Duino Elegies* at the castle, where he often stayed as a guest of Princess Maria von Thurn und Taxis-Hohenlohe.

NEW POEMS (1907–1908). Rodin's impact on Rilke was profound. The poet's writing up to the point of his contact with Rodin had been relatively abstract, and his method of work was reliant on spontaneous inspiration. Rodin's art, on the other hand, was concrete; he was a workman, showing up in the studio and getting right to work and forcing inspiration to come to him. Rilke strove to adopt this new work ethic and to write a more "sculptural," naturalistic type of poetry. The result was what Rilke called *Dinggedichte,* or "thing poems." These thing poems do not quite represent William Carlos Williams's later maxim, "No ideas but in things," but they are certainly more object oriented than anything found in *The Book of Hours* and are filled with descriptions of places, animals, and people. In one of the more famous poems from this collection, "The Panther," the big feline paces empty eyed in its little space behind the bars of its zoo paddock. Even at this stage Rilke is already poised for *Duino Elegies,* as is apparent in "The Angel": "With a slight tilt of his brow he rejects / everything that limits and obliges; / for the wide circles of the eternal Coming / pulse hugely uplifted through his heart."

Resources

Almost all of the collections and archives devoted to Rilke's life and work are located in Europe, mainly in Switzerland and Germany.

German Literature Archive. This archive, in Marbach, Germany, houses a Rilke collection and maintains a Web site (only in German, unfortunately) (www.dla-marbach.de).

International Rilke Society. This society, based in Switzerland, publishes the journal *Blätter der Rilke-Gesellschaft* and sponsors international conferences, with Rilke as the focal point of more general scholarship on the arts, history, and humanities. It also maintains a Web site (www.rilke.ch).

Rainer Maria Rilke Museum. This museum, located at Rue du Bourg 30, 396 Sierre, Switzerland, near Rilke's Château du Muzot, holds a remarkable collection of photos, manuscripts, letters, and numerous other documents. As of 2003 the museum did not have a Web site, but that situation may well change.

Swiss National Library. The Swiss National Library, in Bern, houses a Rilke collection as part of its literary archive. Though the museum has a Web site accessible to English speakers (http://www.snl.ch/e/aktuell/index.htm), the section of the site that concerns the collections is available only in French and German.

University of Kansas. The German libraries at the university, located in Lawrence, Kansas, house a Rilke collection that consists of 1,200 first-edition volumes of Rilke's work.

HEATHER MCCLOUD-HUFF
MICHAEL HUFF

Index

Page numbers in **boldface** type indicate article titles. Page numbers in *italic* type indicate illustrations.